T0300456

Routledge Revivals

Rationalisation and Unemployment

First published in 1930, John Hobson's study deals with the economic dilemmas generated in the early twentieth century by the advent of mass production. Namely the over-production and surfeit of goods and the resultant failure of the expansion of markets leading to record levels of mass unemployment.

Seeking a solution to this dilemma, Hobson analyses all aspects of the problem: income, uses of the surplus, underconsumption, markets and distribution, and internationalism. The study also explores theories concerning economies of rationalisation, both in terms of productivity and consumption.

Rationalisation and Unemployment

An Economic Dilemma

J. A. Hobson

Routledge
Taylor & Francis Group

First published in 1930
by George Allen & Unwin

This edition first published in 2011 by Routledge
2 Park Square, Milton Park, Abingdon, Oxon, OX14 4RN

Simultaneously published in the USA and Canada
by Routledge
711 Third Avenue, New York, NY 10017

Routledge is an imprint of the Taylor & Francis Group, an informa business

Publisher's Note
The publisher has gone to great lengths to ensure the quality of this
reprint but points out that some imperfections in the original copies may
be apparent.

Disclaimer
The publisher has made every effort to trace copyright holders and
welcomes correspondence from those they have been unable to contact.

A Library of Congress record exists under LC Control Number:
agr31000294

ISBN 13: 978-0-415-68786-7 (hbk)
ISBN 13: 978-0-203-35754-5 (ebk)

RATIONALISATION AND UNEMPLOYMENT

J. A. HOBSON

RATIONALISATION AND UNEMPLOYMENT

AN
ECONOMIC DILEMMA

LONDON
GEORGE ALLEN & UNWIN LTD
MUSEUM STREET

FIRST PUBLISHED IN 1930

PREFACE

LET me state briefly the challenge which the present economic situation offers to the reason of mankind. Recent improvements in the technique and organisation of industry have made it possible to produce, with a given quantity of human effort, an enormously greater quantity of most kinds of goods and devices required for human consumption. This applies not only to most manufactured goods and the machines used in manufacturing processes, but to transport, mining, and many sorts of agriculture. It is manifest that this modern form of producing wealth is outrunning the power to purchase and consume it. For we are confronted, either by actual gluts of goods, such as wheat, cotton, wool, coal, or by stoppages of production due to knowledge that the goods which could be produced by a full use of the instruments of production could not find a market at a price that would cover costs.

It is sometimes sought to evade the issue by describing it as misdirection of productive powers, too much put into some industries, too little into others. But such errors of misdirection are normal waste in the working of the industrial system, and do not account for the abnormality of the present situation. There are no considerable branches of industry undersupplied with the plant and labour needed for productive operations, or unable to get further investment capital or bank advances, provided they can bring good evidence that the goods they can produce can find a profitable market. The excess of productive power is general and is clearly visible in the under-employment of capital and labour in most of the advanced industrial countries. Almost everywhere productive power is held in leash, everywhere unemployed labour confronts un-employed machinery and other 'capital', because markets are not sufficiently expansive to purchase either the consumable goods or the capital-goods which could be produced.

This failure of the expansion of markets is manifestly the crux of the situation. It cannot easily be attributed to a lack of purchasing power. For the income paid in rent, wages, interest, profits, salaries, in the various processes of producing wealth ought *prima facie*, when added up, to make the sum needed to purchase all the goods, if it is used without undue delay in buying goods, the only use to which it can be put.

How little the absurdity of this situation is realised may be gauged by the ordinary man's insistence that all that is needed is higher pro-ductivity, when it should be evident that existing productivity is excessive. It is right, however, to qualify this statement by admitting that increased productivity in one country, e.g. England, if it could be brought about by economies of 'rationalisation', might enable our industries to take away some of the trade done by foreigners in the world-market—that is, to transfer some of our unemployment to these foreign countries. But such rationalisation is a precarious remedy for our unemployment. Its first effect, as shown by statistics, is to 'save' labour—that is, to create more unemployment; and whether its second or third effects will compensate this first seems very dubious, depending very largely upon the competitive reaction of other industrial countries to our policy. Living, as we do, in intimate contact with world-industry and world-markets, the only satisfactory escape from our present plight can be achieved by such improvements in the general distribution of income here and throughout the economic system as will place an increased proportion of the purchasing power in the hands of those who will use them in a general raising of the standard of life of the community. A better distribution and utilisation of income is the only remedy for this failure of expansion of markets, or under-consumption, which shows itself as the direct cause of under-production and unemployment.

This book is intended to establish the argument here outlined in brief.

J. A. HOBSON

HAMPSTEAD
June 1930

CONTENTS

RATIONALISATION AND UNEMPLOYMENT

CHAPTER I

INCOME, MONETARY AND REAL

§ In order to study the tangled issues of rationalisation and unemployment with any hope of
success, it is indispensable that we should get
a clearer understanding of the meanings of the
term income than commonly prevails. For
though income is usually conceived and expressed in terms of money, nobody except a
miser wants money for its sake or would work
to get it. Everyone is after the goods and services
which money will buy for them, now or in the
future, the 'real income'. But the same goods
and services are more useful in some hands
than others, at some times than others, and
thus by their use or consumption confer more
benefit or welfare. So behind the money income and the real income stands the 'vital
income'.

In approaching income by its origins, it is
most convenient to enter by the monetary door.
For in ordinary use income means the money
received by the owners of the requisites of production of saleable goods and services for the

use of these requisites, which are usually classed under the following four heads:—

(1) Natural Resources (land, water, climate, situation, etc.), so far as they yield the materials and energy for helping to produce saleable goods and services, are limited in quantity, and are 'owned'. The income received for the use of natural resources is called Rent.

(2) Capital (machinery and tools, buildings, transport apparatus, mines, and other improvements and developments of natural resources, stocks of raw materials, and stocks of semi-manufactured and fully manufactured goods, gold and other instruments of commerce so far as they assist the sale of goods and services). Goodwill, customary control of a market, credit facilities, and other 'intangible assets' may be reckoned in the 'capital' of a particular business, or even of a nation's business, so far as they are conducive to a money-income for this business. But the amount of this contribution to the aggregate income of the whole economic community is small. The income paid to owners of Capital for its use is sometimes called Interest, sometimes Dividend, and is paid out of a fund called profit. The nature of profit is much disputed. If we ask "What is the requisite of production for which profit is payment?" no clear answer is available. The fact is that profit is essentially that part of the gross income, or receipts, of a business which

remains after the primary expenses of production have been paid out of the sums received for the sale of the goods or services produced by the business. These expenses of production are the overhead expenses, the running expenses, cost of labour (including superintendence and management), materials, power, maintenance and repair of plant, and debenture interest. The owners of the share capital of a modern business are supposed to meet these expenses out of the gross income of the business, before receiving any dividends as payment for their share capital. This residue, i.e. the surplus of the money received for the sale of the product over the expenses of production, is net profit, available either for dividend or for 'reserves', increasing the capital of the business, or safeguarding future dividend payments against 'bad times'. The net profits thus paid out as dividends may greatly exceed the rates of payment for hiring debenture or other fixed interest bonds used in financing businesses. But they carry risks not incurred by any other participants in the business.

Whether 'profits' contain an unnecessary or excessive payment under our capitalist system is a disputed question. Conservative economists represent the whole of surplus profits (i.e. profit above the market rate of interest) as payments for the services of initiative, enterprise, risk taking, and point to the losses incurred in many such investments. Sound speculative judgment, backed by monetary investment, causes real capital and labour to be employed in businesses whose superior productivity and social utility are attested by their high yield of profit. Those who take this view commonly hold that, as payment for skilled judgment and enterprise, profits are not excessive and tend to disappear when others, encouraged by the high gain, enter the field and compete.

Critics of Capitalism find in profits a normal gain coming to owners of share capital by buying manual or brain labour cheap and selling its products dear. That is to say, they regard the condition of the market for labour as generally favourable to the 'Capitalist' buyer, while the market for his product is favourable to him as seller. In other words, profit is gain from processes of marketing in which the organised capitalist-employer has the advantage of being the stronger bargainer. The extreme case is when, alone or by combination with his fellows, he can 'control' a market. But any superiority of bargaining power, either in the purchase of some factor of production or in the sale of its product, yields profit, unless it is offset by some corresponding disadvantage, as, for instance, a rise of rent which may eat up the potential profits of a farmer or a shopkeeper. Where control of superior natural resources is an element in business success, as in the American Steel Trust and many other metal businesses, it is impossible to distinguish what economists term 'economic rent' from other advantages in organisation or marketing which make the business profitable.

But whether profits be attributed to the skill, judgment, and enterprise of *entrepreneurs* and investors, or to control of markets by monopoly or other forms of bargaining, or to possession of superior natural resources, or to hazard, they are distinguished from other sorts of income by the size and rapidity of their expansion and shrinkage. Most other incomes are *relatively* stable; profits peculiarly reflect the prosperous or adverse conditions of trade. Moreover, profits do not appear to be necessary costs of production, but rank as surplus after capital, labour, and ability are paid their subsistence wage.

(3) Brain-labour of invention and discovery, finance and administration of business, the professions and the fine arts, recreations and amusements so far as they are monetary propositions, and involve skilled personal services. The income received for them is composed of salaries, fees, royalties, etc.

(4) Wage-earning labour, manual or mental (no clear division is feasible), and labour of a similar kind done by peasants and individual craftsmen for an income which may or may not

come to them in money. All such incomes may be classed as wages.

None of our divisions of income is watertight, as can easily be seen. Rent at places merges into profit, while interest, salaries, or professional fees may contain elements of profit; wages may absorb some quasi-monopoly gains in sheltered or well-managed trades. In dealing with the use and disposition of the general income we shall have occasion to take note of this over-lapping. But in laying out a ground-plan of the economic system, it is convenient to defer to the accepted general distinctions, classifying the money-income as rent, interest, salaries, wages, profits.

§ From money-income we now turn to the actual goods and services in the sale or purchase of which this money-income is employed and from the production of which it emerges. This is termed the 'real' income. Now money-income may be said to have a double correspondence to real income. First, it is distributed as payment to the several owners of the factors of production in the various stages of production, for productive services actually rendered or as profit. Secondly, it is applied to the purchase of these goods or products, either in their completed state of con-sumable commodities or in their interim stages, as materials or instruments of production. This

use of money-income to buy goods may, however, be delayed, as we shall see, by hoarding
or by a slowing down in the processes of investment, often with injurious reactions upon trade
and employment.

Let me make these statements clearer. As the
processes of converting raw materials into finished
goods, whether for human consumption or for
utilisation in production, are carried on in the
business world, money is concurrently distributed
(at various intervals, from daily wages to half-
yearly dividends) to the persons who apply their
labour, ability, land, capital, in the different
productive processes, or as profit. These payments proceed *pari passu* with the productive
processes, and, as wages, interest, salaries, rents,
or profits, constitute the costs or expenses of
production, on the one hand, and the 'income'
of the recipients, on the other. If, as I urge, it is
convenient to include profit among these expenses, the whole set of payments amounts to
the selling price.

So regarding it, we may say that this selling
price has been paid away in the various expenses
of production. Those who have received these
payments in their money-incomes possess the
wherewithal to buy all the product, alike the
consumable part of it and the capital goods that
constitute the other part.

§ These products may be said to constitute the real income of the economic community, and all the payments made to their producers the money-income. But this is not so simple as it sounds. A large part of the productive activity in a progressive community, the whole in a static community (fixed in numbers and standards of living), is expressed in costs of maintenance, i.e. repair, replacement of wear and tear in plant and tools, and in stocks of materials at different stages of production in the hands of farmers, manufacturers, distributors. This part of production maintains the capital fabric of the economic system. This activity is, therefore, that of mere maintenance. But it is not so 'static' as it seems. For the maintenance is that of an active flow. The process not merely replaces the wear and tear of plant and maintains stocks of materials, it also maintains the normal flow of consumable goods which pass out in retail purchase to consumers. This also belongs to economic maintenance. For the consumable goods which thus flow out in consumption that goes to maintain the energy of the workers and to enable them to replace their wear and tear by bringing up a sufficient family, clearly corresponds to the products that constitute the maintenance of capital. When the economic system is taken as a whole, the payments made to the makers of capital goods needed to main-

tain the capital fabric correspond to the payments made to those producing the maintenance
fund for labour. So likewise, from the standpoint
of an individual manufacturer, his outlay on the
maintenance of his capital fabric corresponds to
his efficiency wage-bill. There is not, indeed, an
exact correspondence. For whereas he must pay
out of his own business resources all that is
necessary to maintain his capital fabric, he need
not always pay out the full cost of maintaining
his labour supply. In a slave economy alone
there is exact correspondence. In the capitalist
system he may be able to draw upon a labour
supply partly financed by the State, philanthropy,
or other trades, contributing to the family upkeep. It may, therefore, sometimes be to his
advantage to pay sweating wages, but never to
let down his capital fabric, unless he is going
out of business.

But apart from this, the fact that the upkeep
of the capital fabric is a charge upon the gross
earnings of a business prior to the earning of a
profit and the payment of interest or dividends,
introduces a disparity in accountancy as regards
the real and the monetary income. In a word,
profits do not bear the same relation to capital
as wages to labour in a business. For, before
profits come into being, a provision for capital
out of gross earnings has been made equivalent
to the subsistence wage paid to labour. This

payment for maintenance of capital does not figure in the net income of the business. Why should it? It is a cost. But so far as it passes in wages and profit to other businesses which make the capital goods bought by the first business for the maintenance of its fabric, it counts in the aggregate income of the economic community.

The importance of this consideration arises from the fact that it invalidates a claim commonly maintained, that in any business the claim of capital to its normal interest or profit stands on the same economic level of necessity as the claim of labour to its subsistence wage. Neither interest nor profit is a necessary payment for the upkeep or maintenance of capital in a going concern, or even in the economic system as a whole. Perhaps this statement needs some modification. For if, after provision for maintenance of capital, there was no fund left for paying interest or dividends, and the future held out no hope of better times, the capital and labour would be let down and the maintenance fund distributed in dividends. In view of this possibility it may be held that some profit is essential to the maintenance of capital, and that, in theory at least, a distinction should be shown between the minimum (rightly regarded as a cost of maintenance) and the rest of the profits. This minimum profit, with the other provision for repair, corresponds to the wage of subsistence.

But it is important to realise that in a particular business the subsistence part of wages stands on the same footing, not with profits, but with the reserve out of which the maintenance of the capital fabric is provided. Nor does this hold good of individual businesses alone. The economic system as a whole, and its constituent industries, must similarly secure the maintenance of their labour supply and that of their real capital, and perhaps the most vital criticism of our existing system is that it makes no adequate direct provision for the maintenance of labour. A slave-owning capitalism would necessarily regard the maintenance of its labour-power as upon the same footing with the maintenance of its plant. But a business that buys its labour-power piecemeal in a 'free' labour market, as it buys its materials and its steam or electric power, need not realise this wider economic necessity.

CHAPTER II

USES OF THE SURPLUS

§ Profits and higher wages (above the current subsistence rate) arise when the economic system, as a whole or in part, produces more goods than are required to provide for its maintenance. It is the causation, distribution, and utilisation of this 'surplus', the fund of progress, that furnish the core of our economic problem. For out of this surplus come the provisions for enlarging the size and improving the productive character of the economic system, so that it can produce an increased quantity and greater variety of goods and services, enlarge leisure, and so raise the standard of living for the same or an increasing population.

In the normal operations of our business system the 'surplus' may take shape in new productive apparatus (increase of capital structure), higher efficiency of labour through rising wages or educational services produced by larger public revenue. The higher standard of working-class living to which higher wages (or shorter hours) and improved public services conduce may not, of course, be represented wholly, or even mainly, in enlarged efficiency of labour, but when it ranks as non-economic welfare it will have a general reaction favourable to the security, regularity, and efficiency of the economic system.

Here we revert to the familiar distinction of the earlier economists between productive and unproductive consumption. The latter, as was recognised by Ricardo, Mill, and others, was not to be condemned, but was in a sense the measure of economic progress, which, after making due provision for improved productivity of the capital and labour structure, could also fructify in providing the economic means of leisure, recreation, and other non-economic activities and enjoyments. Moreover, it was recognised that any surplus not devoted to these sound uses ran to the waste of maintaining an idle rich class in luxury.

§ It is evident that here we enter some vitally important fields of controversy, as to the right proportions of the economic surplus distributed (a) between savings and spendings, (b) between public and private expenditure, (c) between productive and non-productive consumption, (d) between sound and unsound forms of non-productive consumption. We have to consider whether the current economic system contains any adequate provisions for a true adjustment of the several claims upon the fund of progress.

Take first the distribution of surplus as between savings and spendings. Here at the outset we encounter a defective conception of the saving process and of the nature of the product contained in this process. What does an economic community, progressive in its standards of production and consumption, require of the available surplus over and above the maintenance level? More and better material equipment, natural and man-made, better organisation for making, moving, and marketing the larger and more varied product, more knowledge, skill, vigour and training, involving a larger outlay of goods and services in providing a larger and more capable personnel.

In order to evoke the productive use of a larger number, or a better quality, or both, of workers by hand and brain, inclusive of the higher grades of inventive and managerial energy, a part of the economic surplus must be employed in producing more and better workers as well as more and better plant. There is a certain amount of choice as to these applications, better machines economising labour, unskilled men and women displacing skilled, and vice versa. Estimates as to the amount of improved efficiency evoked and maintained by higher real wages, salaries, or profits belong to this section of our enquiry.

The proposed treatment of human and non-human productive resources in one category as regards maintenance and growth involves some changes in economic conceptions relating

to wages, salaries, etc. Whereas, in a mechanical or even a distinctively organic economy, the provisions for maintenance and growth proceed by laws equally applicable to the human and non-human factors, the mental and moral elements in man introduce considerations which have caused economists to disregard these common laws, to which man as an organic structure conforms. In a slave system, where the owners could work their slaves like their oxen and their horses, the distinctively biological character of the economy would be evident, and economic maintenance and progress would be distinguished by estimates of the food and other material provisions required for maintaining and enlarging the numbers and efficiency of the 'human machines'. Costs of maintenance and of progress would be matters of biological calculation, as applied to workers, animals, and crops. In a more or less free community the physiological conditions remain fundamental. A static efficiency requires a certain intake of food and other physical provisions: an improvement of these conditions enables more work to be done; a larger output. But the intelligence and will of the worker, his customary uses of food and other material conditions, his capacity for varying and improving these uses, have an important bearing upon costs of maintenance, and a still more important bearing upon the increased efficiency

evoked by the utilisation of such elements of surplus as come to him in wages that exceed the level of bare subsistence.

But this difference in the motivation of human and non-human factors does not warrant the premature severance of the two in economic analysis. Because human use and enjoyment are the sole and final ends for economic processes, this truth does not warrant us in refusing to recognise the common laws of production and of marketing in which labour and every form of mental energy figure as 'commodities'. The resentment of this 'commodity' treatment of labour by workers has been a source of grave misunderstanding, which has often damaged the presentation of their case for a larger share in the control and the product of industry. For though the sale of labour-power carries human implications which do not apply in other markets, this consideration does not properly enter into the primary analysis of supply and demand.

§ The utility of treating the human and non-human sources of production in the same category is corroborated by the light it throws upon the processes of spending and saving. That surplus which is applied to the enlargement and improvement of the material factors, the development of material resources, improved technical equipment in the shape of power, plant, and materials

is designated 'savings', and has acquired a unique prestige in the economy of economic progress. It is, however, exceedingly important that surplus applied to improve the diet, housing, education, and other elements of economic efficiency of brain and hand workers should be reckoned in this same category of savings. The term should be extended to include all additions to human powers of production made out of the utilisation either of private incomes or of public revenue.

Now the undue concentration upon the saving represented by enlargement and improvement of material capital and the neglect of the saving represented in enlarged and improved labour capacity constitute a chief defect in the operation of modern Capitalism and in the economic thinking formed by it. This defect is natural and inherent in a system wherein each independent productive business comes into being and functions as the property of those persons who own the capital and regard the business exclusively from the standpoint of the gains which come to them as owners, either paid out in dividends or utilised for the improvement of their property.

There is, therefore, an *a priori* probability that too much of the surplus product will take shape in improvement and enlargement of the capital factor of the economic system; too little in the improvement and enlargement of the labour factor. It will, I think, be commonly admitted that, if a larger part of the surplus of English nineteenth-century industry and commerce had passed, either through higher wages or larger and better-expended public revenue, into higher education and scientific research, better housing, food, and general hygiene, our people would now have been in a stronger position to hold their own in the new economic situation of the world. The rapid advance of the United States is manifestly due to the larger share of the surplus which, through higher wages, private benefactions, or public expenditure, has gone into improved human equipment for industry.

A too materialistic view of the economic system means that too much of the progress fund passes into more and better material instruments of production, too little into more and better human instruments. This is evidently detrimental to enlarged productivity, which requires labourers better equipped in hand and brain to operate the larger and better plants.

In estimating the forms and uses of 'saving', sufficient attention is not paid to these considerations. First, the increasing proportion of businesses in the hand of joint-stock companies means that a larger proportion of the national saving is incorporated in 'reserves' or undistributed profits. The portion of such reserves which forms costs of maintenance is, of course, not 'saving' in the sense here given to the term.

But where maintenance is achieved by replacement of worn-out or antiquated plant and other material technique the expenditure upon replacement will frequently contain an enlargement of productive power, better or more labour-saving plant taking the place of inferior plant. Again, 'reserves' in many cases contain large provisions for expansion, often concealed for obvious reasons under the guise of provisions against bad trade. Such saving does not go through any immediate form of non-expenditure and investment of personal income, though it may mature later on in dividends and bonus shares.[1]

In Germany and America more thought and organised support have been given to the combination of progress in material and human equipment than in this country. But the capitalist system, as we see, is in its normal structure and operation ill-adapted for maintaining a right adjustment between the two sorts of saving. For since the 'owners' of the share-capital are the sole owners of the business and the legal possessors of any surplus that may accrue from its working, it is natural enough that they should seek to 'realise' that surplus in provisions that add to the material equipment and value of their property. If a business or a whole trade became a genuinely self-governing corporation,

---

[1] The question how far such elements of saving escape, or are liable to, income-tax does not here arise.

with a due representation of brain and hand workers in the government, the question of the economically right apportionment of surplus as between the owners of capital and the employees in the business, so as to secure that improved productivity which was their common interest, would become a subject of skilled calculation. In the present condition of Capitalism there is nothing to secure that, either directly or indirectly, a sufficient provision is made for improved efficiency of employees to keep pace with the advances in material equipment. The question of numbers comes in here. There is often discovered a deficiency of trained, skilled workers for new or rapidly advancing trades. Professional or trade-union policy is often responsible in part for such a deficiency, for restriction means a temporary gain for the qualified few at the cost of trade development and society at large. There exists no adequate economic machinery for regulating the right apportionment of the fund of progress, or for preventing it passing into stagnant pools or dissipating its productive energy in wasteful expenditure.

§ English economists for the most part have followed and accepted this business view that material savings are the key to economic progress, and that any condition favourable to the increase of such savings in relation to expenditure

upon consumable goods is economically sound.
This has led them to condone, or even to com-
mend, the distribution of the surplus on an
unequal or even an 'inequitable' basis, because
such inequality or inequity puts a larger proportion of the surplus into the hands of a few rich
whose standard of living is so high that they save
and invest what they cannot spend so as to
enlarge their current satisfaction. It seems to
follow from this view that every approach
towards greater equalisation of incomes would
reduce the saving fund, because more of the
surplus would be consumed in raising the current
standard of living of the working population as a
whole. This conclusion is doubly vicious. In the
first place, it disregards the enhanced productivity of the better balance between the material
and human equipment of economic progress that
would result from diverting some surplus profits
into higher wages and salaries. In the second
place, it confuses savings as an amount with
savings as a proportion of the total income or
product.

   If, as it is reasonable to hold, a better or more
equal distribution of income means a better
apportionment of surplus between owners of
capital and employees, and therefore between
growth of capital equipment and of human efficiency, two advantageous results would follow.
In the first place, the aggregate of productive

power would be increased, because of the better adjustment between material and human equipment. In the second place, a fuller utilisation of both material and human equipment would secure a larger total product or real income. For the savings which go into enlarged and improved standards of living for the workers will involve that expansion of markets for consumable commodities, and therefore for the instruments of their production, which is now clearly perceived as the prime desideratum of prosperity. It is now a generally accepted truth that in organised industry[1] there exists a general excess of productive power, in the sense that any attempt to operate this power at its full capacity, so as to produce goods as fast as they can be produced, is soon checked by a failure of markets, followed by a suspension or restriction of productive activity. This is the necessary effect of a distribution of the surplus which induces attempts to increase material capital at a faster rate than human consuming power. A better or more equal distribution of money-incomes would cause a smaller proportion of the surplus to be 'saved' in the narrow sense of savings, a larger proportion to be spent in raising standards of living. So far as the spending went to increased efficiency of labour, it would enhance the productivity of

---

[1] In the United States agriculture is so highly mechanised that it must be included.

industry, though it reduced the *proportion* of the
surplus applied to material apparatus. For the
larger market for final commodities would give
fuller employment to the whole productive
system. There would be an enlarged total product, and though an increased *proportion* of this
enlarged income were 'spent', and a smaller *proportion* 'saved' (in the narrow meaning of the
term), the actual volume of human and material
savings would be greater than before. There is a
double waste caused by the absence of any sufficient
regulation of the saving process. A great deal of
actual savings stored in plant and other capital
is found excessive, and is kept idle or under-
operated for considerable stretches of time. Again,
a great deal of the material equipment, real
savings, which would be produced if there were
reason to believe it could be operated, is not
produced.

It is this last effect of ill-adjusted distribution
that is the chief efficient cause of unemployment.
Since all money-incomes are payments to the
owners of factors of production for the services of
these productive factors, it appears evident that
the adequate power to purchase all goods and
services is created simultaneously with their production. Throughout all processes of production
there is distributed the money that can buy what
is produced. Since this money-income can only
be utilised to purchase products, either con-

sumables or capital goods, why should there
arise any such failure of markets to keep pace with
the expansion of production as actually takes
place? In modern industrial society there is no
wish to keep more money idle, in men's pockets
or in their bank accounts, than is required for
the normal conveniences of economic life. It
might, therefore, be assumed that all incomes
when received would without much delay be
employed either in buying consumables (spending) or in buying capital goods (saving). From
the immediate standpoint of employment and
economic activity it would seem to make no
difference how much of this expenditure went
to buying consumables or to buying capital goods.
There must always be available enough purchasing power to purchase everything that is
produced. The money-income should be con-
vertible into its equivalent in goods, for this is its
sole *raison d'être*. It is, indeed, sometimes objected
that since the output of finished goods (either
consumables or saleable capital goods) follows at
a considerable interval of time the distribution
of their monetary costs in the earlier stages of
their production, a rise in prices may make it
impossible for those paid for production before
this rise took place to buy their proper share of
the whole output. But those who argue thus
forget that the rise of prices supposed to bring
about this *impasse* must itself be due, either to

an actual fall off in supply, or to an increase in monetary demand.[1] In neither case can it be attributed to a deficiency of purchasing power.

Since the monetary payments in productive processes are simply orders upon the general supply of goods, while the process of making these real and monetary incomes is a continuous one, there seems no obvious reason why everything that can be produced should not be produced and find its market by the simple process of converting the money-income into its real equivalents. The fact that this does not happen, that large wastes of unemployment in capital and labour occur, is evidently due to miscalculations in the application of purchasing power. For the smooth conversion of money-income into real income by market purchases implies a correct business forecast of the apportionment of money-incomes among the various sorts and classes of purchasable goods and services. Any great distubance of the economic system, such as took place during the Great War, when the application of purchasing power expanded the demand for certain classes of goods, depressing the demand for others, must leave an excessive apparatus of production in some industries, such as steel and iron, shipbuilding, etc., a defective apparatus in

[1] The relevant consideration that some purchasing power is created not by payments to owners of factors of production, but by banks in the form of credits, is best reserved for discussion a little later on.

others, such as building, and, bringing altera-
tions in the flow of foreign trade, cause much
unemployment in large areas, national or other.
A certain amount of such dislocation, or waste,
must even in normal times occur in a progressive
community, because of the inability to forecast
with accuracy the future changes in the application of money-incomes in demand for the
various classes of commodities or capital goods.

§ But apart from the numerous minor fluctuations in trade, which account for a certain amount
of waste of productive power, there is the major
problem of what is termed cyclical unemployment. This is a somewhat deceptive term to
describe the natural and normal consequence of
an attempt on the part of the industrial community to apply to the purchase of capital goods
and the operation of the 'Capitalist System' as a
whole, a larger proportion of the current money-
income than can find profitable or useful employment therein.

In what may be termed the normal adjust-
ments of the economic system, the quantity of
different sorts of productive energy, applied to
the different processes of the several industries, is
regulated by 'intelligent anticipation' of how the
total volume of purchasing power is likely to be
applied when the goods (consumable or capital)
reach a saleable form. But the question arises, are

there any reasons why business calculations should tend to put more 'saving' into the economic system than can find full employment? And if such a tendency exists, does it account adequately for the waste of unemployment?

§ Now, taking the first question, I think that the urge of 'Capitalism' in our economic system, the facts that business is run by the owners of share-capital for the highest profit, and that a comparatively small proportion of the community are large owners of capital, carry a natural tendency towards the accumulation of new capital beyond the requirements of that economic system as a whole. One aspect of this has already been mentioned, the tendency to put too much of the improvement fund (savings) into the enlargement and betterment of plant and other material capital, and too little into the improved efficiency of brain and manual labour. The placing of large portions of profits to reserves, and the almost automatic saving of large parts of the surplus private incomes from dividends and rents, are not based upon any close consideration of the capital needs of industry as a whole. They are the formal register of the running of industry in the sole interests of the owning share-holders, and not of the whole body of active co-operant agents in the several businesses. Though some qualification of this statement may be found in the alleged disposition of Big Business, especially in America, to introduce an element of public service and workers' welfare into the operation of the business, ignoring or mitigating the legal obligation to run the business on a basis of maximum profits, the general statement still holds good. The fact that the profits of a successful business belong entirely to the owners of the share-capital, and that normally there is no provision whereby the active agents in production, or the consumers who constitute the market for the product, share, either in the conduct of the business or in its profits, causes an excessive proportion of the profits to take the shape of additional plant, materials, and other forms of physical capital. This 'excess' is attested by the inability of the enlarged instrumental capital to operate for any length of time without a stoppage or a slowing down. Thus the capitalist structure of business in an era when new instrumental capital, owing to rapid technical advances, accumulates a higher productivity per unit, makes for a rate of potential productivity more rapid than the rate of effective demand for the final product.

If this analysis of the tendency of capitalist business is correct, it must inevitably cause large fluctuations in the volume of employment of capital and labour. For, just as a maladjustment of the application of new money savings as between the various orders of investment must cause waste by the attempted excessive growth of some and the repression of others, so a larger waste will arise from a normal attempt to put too much of a general surplus of money-income into the enlargement and improvement of the capital factor, too little into the improvement of the human factor. This is an attempt to oversave, in the narrow sense of saving, by overfeeding material capital and underfeeding human efficiency. Let us see just how it must operate. The normal working of the business system everywhere is guided by forecasts relating to the volume of trade and the prices of the articles produced. These forecasts are checked by actual records of sales and prices. When trade is generally improving, and there seem grounds for believing that both the volume of sales and the volume of prices will rise farther, finding fuller profitable employment for the remaining margin of un- or half-employed plant and labour, the stimulus of this trade-prospect will operate first in the fundamental and instrumental trades which provide the plant and the materials for the later manufacturing and commercial processes. The growing profits of improving trades (increased by the lag in wage-rises) will be applied largely in developing and improving the plant and material requirements in these trades, and large bank advances will be available for running expenses. This calculation will for a time be justified.

The increased activity arising from the belief in further trade prosperity will have its natural effect in stimulating activity in the later productive processes which will purchase and operate the increased plant which the instrumental trades are producing, so as to expand the aggregate productive power at those stages, and take advantage of the expansion of markets and rises of prices which are taking place and are expected to continue. This is the familiar movement in a trade recovery. So long as the expectation of increasing prosperity is fulfilled by the fuller employment of existing plant and labour, and the larger volume of sales at rising prices, large reserves and a large part of the high dividends of prospering businesses are employed in the enlargement and improvement of the capital structure of businesses. When this increased productive activity has gone so far as to absorb the whole of the available labour, the influence of the boom confidence continues for a time to produce a speculative promotion of industrial companies and a speculative purchase of goods for later profitable selling at the higher prices believed to be attainable. But it presently becomes evident that the enlarged productive power, both instrumental and manufacturing, is excessive, in the sense that its full product cannot be marketed except at such a fall of prices as leaves no margin of profit. This discovery is made public by the actual fall of selling prices, which rapidly causes banks to restrict their credits and call in their loans, compelling businesses to reduce their production and their employment of labour.

Both plant and labour are now reduced to idleness, a waste due to an attempt to force production to a point beyond the possibility of profitable marketing, or, in other words, an attempt to apply to increase of producing power in capital an excessive proportion of the money surplus after money costs are met. That this is so appears from the failure of would-be 'savers' to effectuate their money savings by converting them into real savings.

§ In the working of a progressive economic system the right understanding of the time element is of paramount importance. Business men, and sometimes economists, speak as if the distribution of money-income was *prior* to the production of the kinds of goods this income was used to purchase. In particular it is represented that money savings effected by a business community are *first* invested and *then* set to order new productive plant and other material capital, including the extra supplies of food, clothing, etc., required to supply the increased body of wage-earners who will operate the increased instrumental capital. But this is not a true account of the 'saving' process. What actually occurs is that in the current operation of business productive energy is applied to the processes of producing new capital goods of various sorts, beyond the needs of capital maintenance, in the calculated expectation that as soon as they are produced they will be bought by the money savings which continuously flow from the incomes that are continuously distributed. Thus the real savings and the money savings designed to purchase them are produced simultaneously. The assumption is that a current accumulation of monetary savings, in the shape of reserved and private investments, will *without delay* purchase and operate the real savings.[1]

§ Now this application of monetary savings to purchase the fresh stocks of real savings without delay notoriously fails when sufficient real capital already exists to assist in producing all the goods which can find a profitable market. When industry does not require more plant, and company promotion flags, the monetary savings, which strictly correspond to the real savings they were

[1] This is the normal procedure. It seems, however, to take no account of new business propositions needing kinds of plant the demand for which could not have been anticipated. What will have been saved in anticipation of such unknown demands is food and other consumables required by the workers who will be set to make the unanticipated plant.

expected to purchase, do not fulfil their expected
part. Money savings, instead of flowing rapidly
through the investment market into the purchase
and operation of the new plant, linger in deposit
accounts at banks, awaiting some recovery of
trade. In other words, there is a slowing-down
of the conversion of monetary into real savings,
with a corresponding check upon the potential
increase of production. When the industrial
system as a whole is working 10 per cent. or 20
per cent. below its normal, this is no time to apply
your money savings to enlarge the scale of
operations. So the failure of money savings
already existent to fulfil their normal function of
buying the plant and other capital goods that
represent real savings checks further waste of over-
production by substituting unemployment.

The money savings no doubt are eventually
attached to real savings through investment, but
the delay in making this attachment is doubly
injurious to trade and employment.[1] The delay

[1] Dr. Cannan regards this eventual absorption of wasted productive power as a 'true remedy'. Reviewing Professor Clay's
The Post-War Unemployment Problem in *The Economic Journal*
(March 1930), he writes: "The true remedy for long-term unemployment, always applied throughout history, and always
effectual, is neither rationalisation nor reduction of wages, but
redistribution of labour-force between the different occupations.
When there are more people offering to do some particular kind
of work than can be employed in it without reducing the advantages much below those of other occupations, surely the obvious
and certain remedy is a redistribution of labour-force in the
shape of a decrease in the number of persons offering to work

in purchasing the plant and other material capital produced in expectation of immediate sale slows down production in the trades making this form of capital. It also postpones the period when material capital gets into operation and affords employment. A third result of this delay is the diminished use of bankers' credit in financing the current expenses of manufacturing and commercial businesses in buying materials and paying wages. A depression thus initiated brings about a fall in rate of profits on a declining volume of trade, and greatly reduces the surplus put to reserves or to investment purposes, while reduced employment, especially in the funda-mental and instrumental industries, curtails the production of the kind of goods which represent

in the depressed trade and an increase of persons working in the others." Obvious and certain remedy, indeed! In a period of general depression what are 'the others'? Dr. Cannan, in assuming that a depression means a misplacement of productive power as between different occupations, misstates the whole problem. In Britain, Germany, and the United States at the present time of depression (1930) there are no substantial trades short of labour, and capable of absorbing for present productive purposes the surplus labour in the great basic occupations where unemployment most prevails.

Eventually, no doubt, the unemployed are for a time absorbed, partly in new or growing industries, partly in the revival of the old industries. But to call this eventual absorption a 'remedy' is a ludicrous misnomer. The disease is allowed to run its course: the full mischief, the waste of existing capital and labour over a period of years, is not prevented or abated by Dr. Cannan's 'effectual' remedy. What is wanted is a remedy *against* unemploy-ment and depression, not a declaration that when the disease has run its course the patient may—or even must—recover!

real savings. Production goes on under depressed conditions, the volume of real savings and of monetary savings is greatly reduced. For a time, in fact, the situation is one of undersaving, in the sense of a rate of current saving lower, both in amount and in proportion to total income, than normally prevails and than is necessary for a progressive economy. Thus an effort in normal and in prosperous times to oversave, in the sense of creating a larger volume of productive capital than can be utilised, is offset by a period of undersaving as a consequence of lowered production.

CHAPTER III

UNDERCONSUMPTION

§ The difficulty in accepting this analysis as correct appears to arise from the following causes. It is easy to understand how, in default of reliable trade statistics, owners of productive businesses and the investing public may make serious and frequent mistakes as to the amount of new capital resources which the prospects of the different industries seem to justify. Some considerable waste, and recurring unemployment from such ignorance and miscalculation, appear natural and inevitable. But that there should be any great maladjustment between the proportion of money-incomes spent in demanding consumable goods as a whole, and the proportion spent in demanding capital goods as a whole, is a proposition very difficult to accept. In spite of a wide consensus of business men as to the growth of an excessive productive power, not in this industry or that, but in industry at large, economists have generally held to the belief that the regulation of the ratio of spending and saving was governed by laws so sound in their operation as to preclude any possibility of applying too much productive power to new capital construction. Any such tendency, they think, would be checked at once and automatically by a fall in interest and profits. Nor can they admit that, even 'in theory', oversaving is possible. For modern science and technique disclose boundless opportunities for the development of natural resources, the improvement of communications, and other material provisions for the more distant ripening of productive resources into consumable goods and services. Since man's future wants are boundless, the provision of capital for satisfying them is similarly boundless.

Yet economists have themselves furnished trenchant criticisms of this supposition of a natural harmony between spending and saving. For they have admitted that, as regulators either of the volume of saving or of its proportion to spending, the rates of interest and profits are extremely defective. For much saving is indeed, regardless of the rate of interest, an almost automatic setting aside of surplus income, while some private saving is even stimulated by a lower rate of interest when the motive of the saving is some fixed provision for the future. It is true that, as has been stated, saving tends to dry up in bad times because the 'surplus' over costs, distributed in interest and profits, is largely reduced. But to remedy oversaving by undersaving is an aggravation of the disease.

Professor Birck, in an interesting discussion of theories of overproduction,[1] finds the chief cause

[1] *Economic Journal*, March 1927.

of modern depressions and unemployment in "a higher technique, not accompanied by a corresponding increase of capital". By this he means that £1,000 of money savings applied to the purchase of improved machines will enable a manufacturer to turn out the same product with the employment of fewer workers than he employed when £1,000 of inferior machines were used. This improved technique, unless accompanied by a great expansion of the use of the improved machines to supply an expanding market, means unemployment and a lower wage-bill. But £1,000 spent in buying the improved machines effects a larger volume of 'real' savings, or productive power, than the same sum formerly spent on buying the inferior machines.

Attention has already been called to this point in dealing with the use of 'reserves' for replacement. If the machines replaced are of a higher productive capacity per £1,000 spent on them, this replacement is not mere maintenance, but contains an element of 'saving' represented by increased productive power of capital. But Professor Birck does not explain why the application of this labour-saving machinery, which lowers the cost of production per unit of the product, does not lead to lower competitive prices and expand the market for the product so as to afford as much employment as before.

The point regarding improved technique is

relevant only as it affects the changing proportion between monetary saving and spending at any given time. In a static condition of the productive arts a larger proportion of the money-income can rightly be absorbed in saving than at a time when new inventions are applied so as to enlarge the productive power attached to each unit of money saving, when converted into real saving.

Professor Birck holds that "inventions are materialising at such a pace that capital accumulation cannot keep pace". But why? Such inventions are economies of saving in that the same amount expended on enlarged equipment (real savings) as before will give a greater addition to the productive power, when its labour-saving economy is taken into consideration.

Again, Professor Birck does not explain why "in the organic composition of capital as it is to-day" there should be "too much of fixed, too little of circulating capital". The rapid growth of inventions is no explanation. That is a generally recognised fact, and would influence real savings in the sense that it would put more of the real savings into the shape of circulating, and less into the shape of fixed capital, in order to retain a right adjustment between the two forms of capital.

§ The part played by bank credits in the provision of running expenses demands examination here. So far as these credits consist of depositors' money put to their accounts in the bank, they represent money savings which are not immediately invested by the 'savers' in purchasing the 'real savings' they represent. The banks, so far as they use these savings as temporary loans to finance trade do, however, convert them into the means of purchasing raw materials and paying wages, i.e. enabling workers to buy food and other necessaries which otherwise they could not have done. Now, these supplies of raw materials, food, etc., have been produced in the expectation that they would be purchased out of the credits thus supplied by banks. In other words, they form part of the real savings normally provided by the economic system for capital uses.

While it is generally recognised that the bulk of purchasing power applicable to the purchase of the product consists of the incomes paid to the owners of the factors of production, misunderstanding sometimes arises with regard to the bank credits employed at the various stages of production, industrial and commercial, for the provision of running expenses. These credits are sometimes regarded as additional volumes of purchasing power created by banks, falling outside the ordinary category of 'costs' of production. The mysterious ways in which these credits are created, increased or contracted, tend to put them outside the ordinary analysis of costs. But closer consideration makes it evident that the bank credit, in its normal operation, must be regarded as an instrument of production, enabling the other instruments to function more freely and productively than otherwise they could. Thus the payments to the banks for the use of credits, enabling them to regulate more freely their purchases of materials and labour, and to hold their stocks, are 'costs' on a level with the other costs of production at the various stages of industry and commerce. These current payments are as much liens upon the goods produced as are wages, salaries, and other incomes paid to suppliers of land, machinery, management, and labour. No inflation or rise of prices is attributable to their normal working. They are payments of income to bank shareholders, clerks, and other persons associated with banking, for services rendered to industry and commerce which are productive in the same sense as are railroads, which assist the movement of goods and thus add to their utility. The fact that sudden increases or decreases of the price of these bank services may exercise a general influence in stimulating or depressing trade, through their effect in raising or lowering the price level, does not differ essentially from the powers vested in transport industries to change their rates for the services they render.

The question whether the important and wide reactions upon the whole of industry and commerce, produced by changes in the bank rate and the supply of monetary services, should be entrusted to ordinary capitalist businesses out for profits, depends upon whether a policy most profitable to the banks normally and necessarily coincides with a policy most serviceable to the industrial community as a whole. If those are right who contend that in certain situations of the trade-cycle well-considered doses of inflation assist the recovery and expansion of production and of commerce, the creation of these additional supplies of money must be held to be a useful operation which deserves payment. Whether the issue of such extra money and the terms exacted for its use should be left to a few bankers, not in any formal sense representative of the business community vitally affected by their conduct, is a question which belongs to the wider problem of the social control of key industries.

Where these increases of credits are of such a nature that they cannot be anticipated by the price activities of the business world, they rank for the time being as pure creations of purchasing power, which stand on an equal footing with the monetary savings of business resources or private citizens. As they compete with these actual monetary savings in the markets for goods and services, they raise prices and enable non-savers to get a portion of the real savings away from savers. In a word, they act in the first instance as inflation. It is, however, claimed that in normal trade this process performs two useful functions: one, that of enabling ordinary traders to economise their own capital resources by expanding or contracting their running expenses according to their changing situations; secondly, that of furnishing a stimulus to productive industry by the very rise of prices due to incipient inflation. This effective stimulus, by increasing the rate of supply of goods, stops at an early stage the rise of prices which is its first effect, and is an instrument of higher productivity and employment. So far as this holds good, the bank-made increases of purchasing power by effective inflation may be regarded as a special form of productive power within the economic system, supplementing the normal interaction between real savings and money savings. Indeed, bearing in mind that normally the apportionment of productive energy is distributed among the different industries by means of an intelligent anticipation of future markets and their prices, it will appear that, if trade prospects are favourable to a state of trade which requires for its financing a larger volume of bank credits, more productive energy will be applied to the production of the kinds of goods which such increased credits will go to purchase. This means that there will be no lack of the raw materials, foods or other 'real' wages, which a free expansion of trade under improved technique and enlarged employment will require. So far as this holds good, it signifies that the increases of bank credits, sometimes called inflation, are operative by anticipation in stimulating the supplies of those sorts of capital goods they are set to buy. *Pro tanto* they do not raise prices in the markets for those goods. Nor can it be maintained that this anticipatory diversion of productive energy into the production of those goods injures production as a whole by restricting the productive energy put into the trades producing plant and other fixed capital, if it be true that, apart from such enlarged credits, there would be a tendency to produce more of the improved machinery than could find profitable employment, owing to the shortage of 'circulating capital'. This attribution of utility to bank credits cannot, however, be taken to imply that a close natural harmony exists between the profitable interests of the banking industry and the interests of economic society as a whole. Indeed, a suspicion of disharmony is aroused by the fact that banking has remained in its highest prosperity during the deepest and most prolonged industrial depression to which our country has ever been subjected. There is the further danger lest the working of a credit-making operation in the direction of inflation may lend itself to injurious modes of speculation either on the Stock Exchange or in the investment market. It is largely owing to this suspicion that the profit-making interests of private bankers may not coincide with the interests of the economic community as a whole that a growing demand arises for a more adequate social control of credit.[1]

§ Summarising the course of our argument thus far, we may say that a rapidly rising technique and improved organisation have undoubtedly led to a rapid increase of the productive power of industry. But the inability to make full profitable use of this increased power must be imputed to a failure to make a full, continuous use of the purchasing power created and distributed simultaneously with every act of production. This failure, again, can only be imputed to a maldistribution of income of such a kind as to place too much purchasing power in the hands of the richer classes, who allow it to accumulate for investment, too little in the hands of those who desire to raise their standard of living. The necessary effect is to evoke a monetary saving which is found to be excessive, in that the increased goods it is intended to produce cannot actually get produced, because there is an insufficient

[1] The dawning recognition of the need of some such social control over the application of new investment capital is to be found in the recent establishment by the Bank of England of an Investment Corporation to advise and direct the flow of new capital.

market for them. A better and more equal distribution of 'surplus' income is thus seen to be necessary to give full continuous employment to capital and labour in an economic system whose productive technique is constantly enlarging the productive powers of the community.

Why should it be so difficult for those who recognise the waste due to ill-considered distribution of savings or investment money as between the instrumental and the final industries (as Mr. D. H. Robertson appears to hold), or between fixed and circulating capital (Professor Birck's contention), to realise the far larger waste that must inevitably occur if it is sought to apply too much income to the purchase of capital goods in general, too little to consumable commodities? Why, further, should it be assumed that a more equal and more equitable distribution of money-income would lead to a deficient growth of capital and disable a community from taking full advantage of new inventions and improvements of technique? The saving of a smaller proportion of a much larger real money-income by a more widely distributed prosperity would be a better guarantee of a harmonious adjustment of production to consumption than the present inequality admits. For, since the inability of the maximum product to get produced is admittedly due to the knowledge that, if produced, it would not be profitably sold, a distribution of purchasing power which would ensure a larger, quicker, and more reliable demand for commodities would maintain the full flow of production and the maximum output.

The confinement of the term 'saving' to the monetary method of enlarging capital has prevented the recognition of the truth that as the first call upon the product is for the maintenance equally of the material and the human productive factors, so also the second call should be equally applicable to both factors. In other words, 'saving' for the enlargement and improvement of productive resources should be represented not only in terms of capital, but in terms of human enlargement of productive power, more and better labour. It would then be clear that larger and better expenditure of the workers must stand on the same level as increased and improved plant, and that a proper proportion between the two uses of savings must be secured. If too much saving is put into enlarged and improved plant, too little into enlarged efficiency of labour, the increased capital is not utilised to its full efficiency, and, as we see, the whole of its possible product cannot be marketed.

§ Neglect of the considerations here set forth has led many economists and business men to express alarm at the post-war extravagance and lack of thrift which they find alike in individual and in

Governmental finance. National savings are a smaller proportion of national income than before the War.

"On the basis of material compiled for the Census of Production, it is estimated that national savings just before the War amounted to from £380 to £400 millions sterling per annum. At the price level of 1925 this would be equivalent to between £600 and £650 millions. Although these figures are subject to an even wider margin of error than the pre-War estimates, they leave no possible doubt that there is a large deficiency of annual savings compared with the period before the War. This deficiency is probably in the neighbourhood of £150 millions."[1]

I should accept this statement of the facts, but with the comment that the term 'deficiency' begs the whole question, suggesting that a larger amount of investment saving could have found lucrative employment in 1925 or in the subsequent years of depression. But there are several other points for criticism in the attitude of economists towards the reduction of investment saving. In the first place, I cite the refusal to count as 'saving' the sums that are represented in raising the standard of efficiency of labour, the higher wages, and the public expenditure that improve the physique, intelligence, and security

[1] Committee on Industry and Trade. Part I of *A Survey of Industry*, p. 55.

of the workman and his family. Some of the reduction of capital-saving has been transformed into improved efficiency of working-class life.

Again, it is well to point out that 1913 was a year of high industrial prosperity, when profits were large and opportunities for further lucrative investments were afforded both in this country and abroad to the well-to-do classes. The period from 1924 onwards has offered few such opportunities, either for attaining high profits, or for their lucrative employment as invested savings. There is thus no warrant for describing the lower rate of saving in 1925 as a 'deficiency'. Moreover, in this Report no allowance is made for the higher physical productivity of £100 of newly purchased plant in 1925 as compared with 1913. Not only does this apply to additional plant and other productive capital, but it means that replacement by means of 'reserves', which is not accounted 'savings', does in fact make large additions to the productive power of capital. Another consideration must not be ignored. The rate of export of British capital, needed for the development of backward countries before the War, was justified by the fact that we had the largest exportable surplus, and that the further development of backward countries was needed to ensure to our growing population the increasing supplies of goods and raw materials essential to our maintenance and industry. Now other countries, and especially America, are able to take a much larger part in world-development than before the War, and are doing so. We can, therefore, reserve for home employment a larger share of our savings, especially in view of the approaching stabilisation of our population, which will not require us to expend so much of our savings in enlarging the foreign supplies of goods and raw materials for home consumption.

Finally, it may be admitted that during recent years there has been 'undersaving' in one sense of that term. The lowered rate of production, relative to our full capacity, during these years has reduced the saveable surplus in the shape of business reserves, high dividends, and middle-class prosperity. Therefore, though the actual rate of savings is adequate to the requirements of our depressed condition, it falls considerably below what could usefully be employed under conditions of revived prosperity. But it is an error to suppose that increased thrift under existing conditions would help to achieve prosperity. On the contrary, the attempt to save a larger proportion of our reduced monetary and real income would worsen the malady by offering for investment more savings than could be digested by the industrial system. As I have stated, there is no shortage of investment capital for any business which can show a sound business proposition with a good prospect of a profitable sale of its

goods. Nor would such a business find any difficulty in getting bank aid for its running expenses.
It is, therefore, wholly unwarranted to maintain
that our lower rate of savings means a 'deficiency'.

§ The notion that, as a nation, we can advan-
tageously save an unlimited proportion of our
national income rests on a fallacious interpretation of our experience during the first half of last
century, when we had the expanding world-
market as our perquisite. Any nation, as any
individual, may save any proportion of his
income he chooses, provided he can get others
to consume the goods his 'savings' are employed
to produce. During the first half or three-
quarters of the nineteenth century this was our
situation. The export trade for manufactures was
mainly in our hands, and its expansion enabled
us to apply to the increased productive plant an
unrestricted share of our national income. But
what a single individual or a single business
group or nation may do is not possible for the
economic system as a whole, nor for a nation
which has lost its relative superiority as com-
petitor for world-markets.

CHAPTER IV

RATIONALISATION AND PRODUCTIVITY

§ Our argument thus far has established two propositions. First, there exists a general tendency in the economic system for the productive capacity to outrun the expansion of markets. Secondly, this is attributable to a distribution of money-income which upsets the true balance between saving and spending, productivity and markets. It is now desirable to relate this argument to the processes included under the term 'Rationalisation', to which many business men, politicians, and economists are looking as a remedy for our present economic troubles. Improved plant and mechanical power, accelerated labour, better organisation of business personnel, and better marketing arrangements are the main factors in rationalisation. A single business in an industry of competing businesses, pursuing such a policy, may effect considerable economies that lead to a reduction in costs of production per unit of its output. If its output was no larger than before, this would mean a reduction in the number of employees. Labour would be 'saved'. But, since a business employing this policy would be able to undersell other competing businesses which carried on in the older wasteful ways, it might take a large enough share of the market to enable it to expand its output sufficiently to employ as many workers as before, or even to increase the number. The displacement of workers would then be thrown upon the other businesses whose markets it had taken. There would probably be some enlargement of total supply and some fall in selling price resulting from this policy. But if a similar rationalisation were not undertaken by the other competing businesses, an expansion of the rationalised business, perhaps accompanied by an absorption of some of the competitors and a suppression of others, would almost necessarily occur. In this way rationalisation usually extends to all or most of the strong businesses in a trade. Indeed, its full economies can only be realised when it signifies organisation of a whole industry for pursuing a common policy in methods of production and marketing. Though early experiments in such an organisation may leave much independence to individual businesses in production and finance, confining their federal policy to agreements upon output and selling prices, the normal development is towards the closer union of a cartel. Now, while there are many differences in the structure and working of cartels, their normal method is the regulation of the total supply in a national or a world-market so as to secure a profitable price, buying up or putting out of business firms with inferior equipment, management, or position, imposing specialisation of productive processes, with organised bulk buying of materials, power, and labour.

Now the first effect of this process carried on in a whole industry is generally understood to be a reduction in the number of workers, i.e. unemployment. Less labour is put into each unit of the product. More use of automatic machinery, higher standardisation, less waste in buying and selling, imply a reduction in employment, especially of the skilled and higher-paid workers. Wages seem hit in three ways: by a reduced number of wage-earners, by a reduced proportion of skilled and relatively highly-paid workers, and by wage-cuts pressed on Trade Unions when weakened by unemployment.

But these bad reactions upon wages and employment are based upon the assumption that the business organisers of this policy will adopt a selling price that will require them to restrict production so as to secure the full gains of their economy in high profits on a limited sale. This, however, is not the necessary effect of a rationalising policy. The large increase of productive power, in the form of capital and better organisation, which attends a successful rationalisation would not be utilised in most industries without an actual enlargement of the product, and this enlargement can only be sold by lowering prices so as to enlarge the market.

This will not apply equally to all cases. Where rationalisation involves no considerable capital expenditure in new plant or other technical improvements, but consists chiefly in economies of a monopolised market, and where, as in the case of some prime requisites of life or trade, the elasticity of demand is low, it may pay a cartel or other combine severely to restrict output and even to raise prices.[1] But more usually mass-production under a cartel policy will find it profitable to increase production by some reduction of selling prices, earning a larger aggregate profit out of a somewhat reduced profit per item of the larger output. In so far as this policy is pursued, the reduction of employment and of the wage-bill will evidently be less than where

[1] Restriction of output, indeed, is regarded as a normal economy in the rationalising process. Lord Melchett, for example, gives it the first place in his analysis. "Basically (writes Lord Melchett), rationalisation is simply the rational control of industry to ensure that as far as possible you do not produce more than your market can absorb. . . . It means the closing down of obsolete plant and machinery and of unprofitable mines and factories, and the allocation of production to those mines and factories most favourably situated and equipped. It involves the use of every labour-saving and every fuel- and power-saving device which, together with the elimination of every unnecessary link in the chain of distribution, results in a vital saving in the ratio of costs to output. It means concentration on scientific research, the employment of the latest plant and inventions, and the scrapping of obsolete equipment. In the purchasing of raw materials, in transport, and in the chain of distribution and of merchanting abroad it means unification and centralisation, with all the corresponding economies and enhanced efficiency."

a more rigorous reduction of output is imposed. Indeed, when the elasticity of demand is great, the whole of the workers who would have been displaced under the former market conditions may be retained, and an addition may be made to the total volume of employment in the trade.

But even where some net reduction of employment and of wages occurs within the rationalised trade, it may be compensated by considerations affecting other workers. When heavy expenditure is incurred in replacement of obsolete or inferior plant a stimulus will be given to employment and wages in metals, machine-making, mining, and other fundamental industries which, though temporary in each case of rationalisation, may count considerably when a more enlightened scrapping policy (on the American scale) comes to be adopted.

Further, when rationalisation is followed by a planned reduction of selling prices to satisfy an expanding market, the real wage throughout the whole consuming community is raised by the fall in price of an item in its standard of living. Even if the product is not itself a final consumable article, but a semi-manufactured article that is utilised in other trades, the lowering of costs of production in these other trades will normally be followed by a reduction of prices in some markets for consumable goods, so raising the purchasing power of a given income. When the product of a rationalised trade is thus sold at a lower price, either that lower price greatly stimulates effective demand (in which case employment and wages in the particular industry may be as high as, or even higher than, before) or else the lower price paid for what is bought may leave a larger quantity of purchasing power available for more demand in other markets, stimulating employment and wages in these.

§ In a word, when considering the effects of rationalisation, we must not confine our attention to the immediate results and the rationalised industry, but to the further effects upon volume of employment and of real wages in the industrial community as a whole. Regarding, as we must, rationalisation as the most recent and progressive type of Capitalism, does its advance in the industrial world, though primarily motived by the pursuit of profits, involve an increase of the rates of real wages and of employment in the rationalised industries and in the economic system as a whole, and in the proportion of the aggregate product which comes directly and indirectly to the wage-earners?

The full validity of rationalisation as a policy for maximising production and raising the general standard of consumption depends upon an adequate expansion of markets. Does this take place? The evidence of the last few years, especially in the United States, where the rationalising process has gone farthest and fastest, does not support a favourable answer to this question. The following table, relating Volumes of Employment, Pay Roll and Production, is based upon Bureau of Labour Statistics in the United States:—

Date	Employment	Pay Roll	Production
1919	100	100	100
1920	103	124	104
1921	82	24	80
1922	90	89	104
1923	104	113	120
1924	95	104	117
1925	95	107	125
1926	96	109	129
1927	92	105	126
1928	89	103	132

Another Table on Recent Economic Changes in the U.S. *Report of the President's Conference on Unemployment* corroborates this tendency. Between 1922 and 1927 the average earnings of factory workers increased at a rate of 2·4 per cent. a year, while output per man employed increased by 3·5 per cent. a year: the profits of industrial corporations during this period increased at a rate of 9 per cent. a year. To this it must be added that the total number of workers in these industries showed a reduction of nearly 10 per cent. The Report of the Committee made the

following comment upon the causes of this
development: "Acceleration rather than struc-
tural change is the key to an understanding of
our recent economic developments. Gradually
the fact emerged in the course of this Survey
that the distinctive character of the years from
1922 to 1929 owes less to fundamental change
than to intensified activity." There is, we are
told, no noticeable trend towards production on
a larger scale. But Mr. P. W. Martin, of the
International Labour Office, comments upon the
American figures in the following terms:—

"On the other hand, while there has been no
extraordinary increase in the average number
of wage-earners per establishment, the average
horse-power has increased from 126·2 in 1914
to 203·4 in 1927. This increase in the amount
of power used, with a concomitant growth in
machinery, accounts, no doubt, for much of the
increase in productive efficiency. But while it is
true that an increased use of power and an
increased use of machinery are major factors in
the increased productivity, they are by no means
the only factors. On every hand there have been
developments in the general technique of production. Machines are made to run faster. One
man is in charge of more machines. There has
been a greater mechanisation of the human factor
itself; the principle of division of labour has been
carried to a point where it might more properly

be termed the principle of the subdivision of labour; and to an increased extent skilled work is done by an unskilled or semi-skilled man using a skilled machine."[1]

§ There are at present no comparable statistics available from Germany and England representing the whole body of manufacturing employment. In certain particular industries, e.g. the boot and shoe trade in this country, the statistics appear to show that in 1924 a smaller number of operatives working a forty-hour week produced a larger number of boots than a greater number of operatives in 1907 working at least fifty hours a week. But no valid conclusions as to the general effect of rationalisation upon employment or wages can be based upon the statistics of a single trade or a single group of trades. For there are trades where labour-saving devices do not produce any considerable expansion of market. Boots seem to be such a trade. Though retail prices show less increase than the average retail price for commodities as compared with the pre-War level, no large expansion of the home market has occurred. Rubber soles are perhaps largely responsible for this. But the export market shows a large actual shrinkage in volume of exports since the War, though the latest figures show some recovery. Here is a case

[1] *The Technique of Balance*, by P. W. Martin. I.L.O. p. 13.

where a net displacement of labour may be attributed to improved machinery and organisation. But, taken by itself, it cannot be regarded as indicative of a reduction in the general volume of employment. For apart from some increase of employment that may have taken place in the shoe-machinery manufacturing and the rubber trade, the reduced proportion of national expenditure on shoes (if it has occurred) will signify some increased expenditure on other articles and increased employment in the trades which have not been taking on labour-saving methods.

It is these indirect effects of labour-saving in particular businesses or trades that preclude us from measuring the general effects upon volume of employment. The broader basis of the American statistics, supported as it is by evidence from other great productive industries such as agriculture and mining, does, however, go far to warrant the conviction that rationalisation is not able to get full play for its economies because of the failure of an adequate expansion of home or foreign markets. Though we have not the same amount of statistical support for the effects of labour-saving rationalisation in Germany[1] and

[1] "In Germany the output of potash was increased between 1921 and 1925 by one-third and the number of workers reduced by one-third; the number of cement undertakings has fallen from 157 in 1913 to 150 in 1928, the persons employed from 25,000 to 18,335, while the output has risen from 6·8 to 7·6 million tons; the number of firms producing pig-iron has dropped

England and other highly industrialised countries, the large and persistent body of unemployment is a powerful *prima facie* testimony to a similar failure of expansion of markets, or, put otherwise, a failure of the application of enough purchasing power to buy the larger output which the 'rationalised' processes could supply. The amazing exhibition of a world economic system which is continually tending to produce too much wheat, wool, cotton, leather, coal, steel, shipping, and the manufactured goods into which these materials and services enter, is testimony to the fundamental irrationality in the economy of rationalisation itself. Everywhere, in most trades, extractive, manufacturing, transport, commercial, so much technical and organising power exists that a large and growing proportion is devoted to producing the bad sort of leisure termed unemployment. Yet, as we have shown, the economic wants of man are illimitable. There are would-be consumers for all the wheat, wool, cotton, steel, and other goods that cannot under existing circumstances get produced. There is not any lack of purchasing power or money to buy these goods. Is there any other possible explanation of this irrationality except a maldistribution of income (purchasing power), which

within the same period from 70 to 48, the number of employees from 27,000 to 21,000, while the tonnage rose from 10,916,000 to 13,089,000." *Quo Vadimus?* by A. Loveday (Economic Intelligence Service of the League of Nations), p. 13.

puts a disproportionate amount in the hands
of those who desire to buy capital goods (to
invest) and are unable to achieve their desire
because the final commodities which these capital
goods are intended to supply cannot secure a
full reliable market owing to the too small share
of the total income vested in the would-be
consumer?

§ The attention given to the post-War dislocation
of finance, industry, and commerce and conse-
quent changes in the relative volume and the
direction of national markets, does not touch the
heart of the problem. Rationalisation is driving
home the truth that our malady is one of distribution of income. For it is clear that rationalisation itself is an aggravation of that malady.
The increased productivity it exhibits is not
merely a 'saving of labour' in the several industries. It is a reduction of the part which labour
plays as a productive agent in respect of the
output and an increase of the parts played by
capital and organising ability. This means that
the distribution of the product tends to give a
larger share as payment to capital and ability,
a smaller to labour. If, as is sometimes the case,
rationalisation is accompanied by a rise of wage-
rates in respect of those employed, this may not
signify any reduction in the absolute amount of
the wage-bill for the business or the trade,

though the higher wage distributed over a
reduced number of employees will signify a less
volume of employment except in cases where a
considerable expansion of the market follows.
It is generally admitted, however, that the first
effect is to reduce employment, and the American
statistics certainly indicate that the elasticity of
demand in rationalised industry, as a whole,
does not compensate this first effect by any
subsequent expansion of markets. Though absolute proof may not be available, the restraints
upon output commonly practised by the most
rationalised industries indicate that it is considered most profitable to keep under-utilised
the full productive powers of capital resources
as well as those of labour, except for short
periods of intense production. This, of course,
is no part of the intention of a cartel or other
closely ordered industry. Such an industry would
like to keep its plant in full employment, substituting the more productive power of its capital
for the relatively low productive power of its
labour. But it can only do this under conditions
of a highly expansive market. Bulk production
of standardised goods can seldom rely upon the
required expansion of market to fulfil this condition. It is generally found more profitable to
make a high rate of profit per unit of a restricted
output. Only in those cases where it is more
profitable for capital to go 'all out' in supplying

new strata of demand in the home consumer and the foreign market can it be maintained that the distribution of the rationalised income is such as to give an increased proportion of the enlarged product to the workers, either in their capacity of producers in the rationalised industry, or as consumers in other industries enjoying an increased purchasing power for their wages.

Defenders of rationalisation and cartel organisation, however, frequently contend that the latter result is a natural and necessary outcome of the process, i.e. that the interests of capital and labour (taking due account of the consumer) are identical. American business men and economists, in spite of the recent financial and industrial collapse, are disposed to hold that the necessary balance between production and consumption is maintained. High wages, instalment selling, 'hand to mouth buying', are adduced as instruments for the maintenance of the balance. The policy of high wages is now widely recognised as a condition of high productivity. Here is the doctrine as set forth by one of the ablest of American economists, Professor Wesley Mitchell.

"To find a market for the wares turned out by mass-production and urged on consumers by national advertising, it is patently necessary to have corresponding purchasing power in the hands of consumers. Since studies of national income have demonstrated that wages constitute by far the largest stream of personal income, it follows that wages per man—or rather, wages per family—must be increased as production is expanded."[1]

By 'consumers' here is signified consumers of final commodities. It is rightly recognised that it is their purchases, and not the purchases of new capital goods by investment, that ultimately regulate the balance. But Professor Mitchell's insistence that "wages must be increased as production is expanded" does not fully meet the needs of the situation as we have seen it. The rise in wages must keep pace with the rise, not in production, but in productive power, if the balance is to be maintained. For we have seen that it is productive power that tends to outrun actual production, and to be held up by periods of un- or under-employment. The relatively high wages of America have admittedly been a stimulative and sustaining force for high productivity. But the statistics we have quoted, and the recent disclosures of great waste, not merely through unemployment, but through the concealed waste of excessive selling-apparatus, indicate that though wage-rates are rising for skilled and unskilled labour, they are not keeping pace with profits in the distribution of the enlarged product. There is an aggregate displacement of labour (i.e. more unemployment) and a reduc-

---

[1] Quoted Martin, p. 17: *The Flaw in the Price System.*

tion in the proportion of high-skilled labour to low-skilled in the advanced and 'rationalised' industries. Final consumption is quite evidently failing to keep full pace with increased capacity for production under the new conditions. It is interesting, however, to observe that the American Committee in their Introductory Report do not recognise this loss of balance.

"Our complex and intricate economic machine can produce, but to keep it producing continually it must be maintained in balance. . . . Once an intermittent starting and stopping of production-consumption was characteristic of the economic situation. It was jerky and unpredictable, and overproduction was followed by a pause for consumption to catch up. For the seven years under survey a more marked balance of production-consumption is evident."

It is amazing that the Committee should have ignored the special set of circumstances which for the post-War period enabled America to maintain for a longer period than usual the 'balance', viz. the recovery of her suspended activities in making and repairing houses, roads, and many sorts of plant, the immense expansion of her foreign loans involving exports of goods, the reconditioning and to a large extent the revictualling of Europe, and the comparative shortage of unskilled labour due to the checks on immigration.

These seven years of high and almost unbroken prosperity are no evidence of any lasting balance. They do not refute the statistical evidence showing the diminishing part played by labour in production, and the diminishing share of the total product going to labour in the rationalised industries. Why should we expect it to be otherwise? In every 'rationalised' plant or industry the advance in productivity is due more to improvements in capital than to any increased efficiency of labour. Capital does relatively more, labour relatively less, when due allowance has been made for all labour expended upon capital improvements. Most of the improvements in capital, as technique and power, 'save' labour, and *pro tanto* reduce its total consuming power.

§ But it may reasonably be urged that the reduction of labour-costs and labour-income in rationalised industries does not signify that labour plays a diminishing part in the total volume of production, or that wages form a diminishing share of the total monetary and real income. On the contrary, in many countries real wages have not only risen, but form a larger part of the total income. "Thus in the United States it is estimated that, despite the decrease in the total number of wage-earners, the proportion of national income earned by them rose from 37 per cent. in 1913 to 38 per cent. in 1925;

the proportion distributed in salaries from 15 per cent. to 18 per cent. The share of rents and royalties fell from 15 to 13 per cent., and of profits from 22 to 20 per cent."[1]

"In the United Kingdom the proportion of home-produced social income going in wages (after allowing for employers' contributions to insurance funds, but not for help and relief from taxation) is estimated to have risen, between 1911 and 1924, from 43 per cent. to 45 per cent., and the proportion of earned income to unearned from 75·5 per cent. to 78 per cent." It is, however, admitted that the fall in prices since 1924 has somewhat reduced the proportion of real wages.

It is also urged that this improvement in the income of the workers, supplemented as it is by public services (insurance, health, pensions, education, recreation, etc.), not only implies an equalising process in distribution of the social income, but removes or abates the tendency to excessive saving that upsets the balance of production-consumption. The wage-earners and lower-salaried classes of the towns, whose incomes have risen, spend a larger and save a smaller part of their incomes than the *rentier*, professional, and other higher classes. Now, so far as this can be considered a lasting change in distribution,

[1] *Quo Vadimus?* by A. Loveday. It is, however, difficult to reconcile these statistics with those of our table on page 68.

placing a larger share of the social income in
the hands of the workers and low-salaried classes,
it exercises a marked effect upon the character
of consumption, and thereby of production. Mr.
Loveday puts the matter thus: "In most industrial countries . . . of total income less is required
for the prime necessities, more is available for
secondary comforts."[1]

§ Our main problem thus finds a new setting in
which the psychology of the consumer, the nature
of the growing needs and desires which arise in
his real income enables him to satisfy, enters in.
If it turns out that an increasing proportion of
the wants which a larger real income enables
him to satisfy are more personal, less standardised,
than the prime necessities, it seems to follow that
mass-mechanical processes of production will be
less able to supply them. The issue is of prime
importance. For rationalising economies depend
upon mass-production, and that depends upon
the willingness of masses of consumers to purchase
the same product, or a few standard types of
product. If, therefore, one of the results of
rationalisation is to enable the mass of the
workers to get most of their standardised necessities cheaper than before, and so permit them
to spend a larger proportion of the same or a

[1] *Quo Vadimus?* p. 10. From this statement he excepts England,
"with its large number of unemployed".

higher money-income upon less standardis-
able goods and services, several consequences
follow.

First, a limit, or at least a brake, is put upon
the rationalising movement. While it is true that
skilled salesmanship may, by exploiting the
imitative instinct and the herd-mind, carry a
high measure of standardisation into the comfort
and luxury trades, the fluctuations of tastes and
fashions in such trades will make the more
expensive types of mechanical rationalisation
less profitable. Even the experience of mind-
standardisation in America shows that salesmanship has its limits. In England the individualism
of tastes and demands in the worker-consumer
would assert itself earlier and more vigorously
in any rising standard of living. But everywhere
where the personal differences and preferences
are able to assert themselves—and this is always
possible when the prime necessities are satisfied—
a strong resistance to standardisation, and therefore to rationalisation, is set up. It may be true
that some of the widest-spread new needs, such
as radios, films, gramophones, motor vehicles,
electric apparatus, are eminently suitable for
rationalisation, and if all, or most of, the new
purchasers rendered possible by a higher income
accept these regularities of form, the rationalising
process, with its reduced use of labour and its
increased use of capital, will carry the labour-

saving economy still farther and expand and perpetuate the problem of unemployment.

But such a development would speedily bring rationalisation itself to an *impasse*. For if all, or most, industries proceeded along this road, reducing labour-costs and increasing the part played by capital and its share of the gain, there would be no adequate scope for the investment of new capital, even in the improved methods of producing rationalised goods and services. Since unemployment of labour would be chronic, there could be no tendency towards a rise of wages, and the demand of the workers for the rationalised goods could not increase. A stabilisation of industry would seem to ensue, except for such rationalised trades as could live upon expanding foreign markets—a process that would only postpone the stoppage of further progress.

CHAPTER V

RATIONALISATION AND CONSUMPTION

§ The advance of the new Capitalism, rationalisation, is seen to be distinctively an economy of labour, a thing desirable in itself. If most types of goods and services needed to satisfy the common needs of men could be supplied by industries in which more capital and less labour were required, the liberation of human time and energy thus achieved would enable all to enjoy leisure for the exercise of the human faculties hitherto cramped or atrophied by long hours of specialised labour. Or, instead of taking all the labour-saving in leisure, they could take it out in demands for goods and services which pleased their tastes and expressed their individuality. This would mean that they set to work some of the labour saved by mechanical technique or rationalisation to carry out tasks intrinsically skilful and interesting. For the expression of unique personality in demand involves personal skill in supply. A machine may turn out suits of clothes of certain standard shapes and sizes, but, since no two persons are exactly alike in shape and taste, an exact fit needs a skilled fitter. And the higher you go in a rising standard of living, the larger the proportion of expenditure conforming to this law.

Thus, rationalisation with its economies adequately used for society would set a natural limit upon its economic function. It would liberate a larger and larger proportion of human time and energy, partly for the demand and supply of goods not conformable to strict rationalisation, partly for leisure and the cultivation of non-economic activities of the mind and body.

§ How far can these gains of rationalisation be got under the existing capitalist regime is a question of supreme interest. Hitherto the advance of Capitalism, though it has brought some improvement of standards of living, some increase of leisure, to the body of the workers, has not secured for them what the better-to-do classes would regard as, in their own case, a tolerable livelihood, and a reasonable share in what makes life worth living. The new Capitalism exhibits immense, almost immeasurable, potentialities of production, everywhere kept in leash by the obvious insufficiency of markets. Can Capitalism itself develop and apply a policy which shall enable the potential market to expand so as to permit it to realise its full economies of production? It is sometimes argued that a sufficiently intelligent Capitalism might come to recognise that its own primary interest, i.e. large profits, required it to encourage an expanding market by a policy of high wages for its employees and of low prices for workers as a whole. Though experience thus far indicates little recognition of any such policy, its advocacy is growing in some quarters. Increased purchasing power by high wages and low prices is seen to be essential to the high regular productivity of rationalised, organised industries. May it not be true that such a policy, affording the fullest productive activity to the largest body of rationalised capital, will yield the largest volume of net profits? If so, reasonable business control will favour a policy which harmonises the interests of capital and labour and secures industrial peace on a basis of high real wages and secure employment. How far is this reasoning valid?

If the economy of rationalisation were consistent with genuine competition between rationalised groups within each industry, prices would fall with the falling costs of unrestricted supply, and the consuming public would secure the gains of cheaper production. The workers in the rationalised groups might obtain relatively high wages, since there need be no reduction in the number employed, and each group would compete with the others in securing the largest volume of reliable and contented workers. But the full economies are seldom achieved by a rationalisation within this competitive order. The process normally signifies the organisation of a Combine, Cartel, or Trust, comprising all the principal productive plants in an industry, eliminating competition in selling prices, and regulating output to maintain a profitable price level. Under such circumstances there is no reason to hold that the consuming public will get in lower prices the whole or, indeed, any considerable part of the gain. The monopoly (for such an organisation is a monopoly) will fix its output and its selling price at such a level as will yield the maximum profit. In order to secure the full economies of rationalisation it may be necessary to increase output, and so to give the consumer some share in the economy of large-scale production. But where, as is usually the case, the existing plant and power can work economically with no such increase of output, no price reduction need occur. The capitalists may secure the whole of the gains in higher profits. But, as in all cases of monopoly, it may be more profitable to take a smaller profit per unit of supply on a larger volume of trade. Here what is termed the elasticity of demand comes in. When the goods in question are a prime necessity of life, or an essential of some important manufacture, it will be more profitable to restrict supply and sell dear, even raising prices above the former competitive level. In such a case the displacement of labour will be at a maximum, and the consumer may lose in high prices part of the purchasing power he formerly applied

to other goods, thus causing loss and unemployment to the trades producing these other
goods.

This is the rationale of the absolute monopoly,
fortunately a rare case. For it is contended that
few Cartels or other rationalised trades are in
such a dictatorial position with regard to the
consumer. Even if there is no direct effective
competition within the Cartel or Combine, there
remains the possibility of outside competition
arising if the Cartel prices and profits are kept
too high. Moreover, there is, in many instances,
competition between goods and services which
satisfy the same sort of want, as between gas,
electricity, and other modes of lighting, heating,
and industrial power. And most articles in the
higher grades of standards of comfort compete
with one another within the expenditure of each
consumer. A notorious example is the effect of
women's smoking in curtailing their expenditure
upon chocolates. The pleasure and the prestige
of owning a motor-car have forced upon large
sections of the public considerable economies in
other articles of consumption, and have shifted
the composition of standards of living. It may,
therefore, be assumed that though the main
incentive and result of the policy is higher profit,
most processes of rationalisation will yield some
gains to the worker-consumer by substituting
mechanical processes for human skill.

§ But there can be no ground for holding that rationalisation as a whole tends to a distribution of income favourable to the workers, either through raising wages or lowering prices. On the contrary, the policy plays in two ways into the hands of Capital: first, by substituting more plant and power for manual labour, and, secondly, by strengthening the Capitalists' power to limit supply and fix selling prices at a level which yields the maximum profits. The consideration that high wages are a necessary condition of expansive markets does not induce any particular rationalised industry to pay higher wages than it needs. For the proportion of such higher wages paid to its workers that would be applied to increased purchases of the particular goods it produced would usually be very small. While, therefore, a general high-wage policy adopted by other trades—raising the general purchasing power of the working-classes—would be useful to the particular industry in the expansion of its market, no separate industry stands to gain by paying higher wages than are necessary to secure the efficient labour it requires. If all rationalised industries could agree upon a wage-raising policy, each might be a gainer by helping to redress the balance between producer and consumer and to secure a general expansion of markets. This is what rationalisation requires for the application of its full economy, but it cannot achieve it by the present separatist method. It cannot, therefore, be held that any natural harmony of interests exists within a rationalised business to secure a large employment at high wages and low prices for consumers.

§ If rationalisation under Capitalism needs to find a social defence, it must adopt another line. And it does. The great corporations, especially in America, sometimes claim voluntarily to adopt the rôle of public services. The shareholders, it is contended, do not control the management of the concerns, so as to insist upon their operation in the exclusive interests of capital. Though the workers in these concerns may have no strong unions to look after their interests, and no effective voice in business control, there is, we are told, a growing disposition to favour policies of high wages, pensions, insurance, and welfare schemes, and to regard the employees as entitled to a share in the prosperity of the business. So, likewise, the growth of this sense of social service impels the management to turn over to the consumer a larger share of the new economies in reduced prices. In a word, we have here the claim that a powerful economic autocracy refuses to regard profit-making as its paramount duty, but, alike in its treatment of its employees and its customers, works in the spirit of a social service. It is Ruskin's doctrine of 'industrial chivalry' rendered plausible, especially in America, by the widespread distrust in governmental controls or in Trade Unionism. Perhaps a deeper interpretation of this 'uplift' or 'social service' propaganda is that, in a country where bureaucracy is at its lowest level of honesty and efficiency, it furnishes a smoke-screen against State Socialism or any other scheme of industrial democracy. It may fairly be admitted that a certain measure of idealism and good will, supported by a sense of the public approval it evokes, tempers the rigour of American Capitalism. But that either in America or in Europe the quasi-monopoly powers wielded by concentrated Capital can be relied upon to serve the interests of employees or consumers, so as to satisfy the demands for a distribution of real incomes adequate to reap for society the full gains of rationalisation, would be a grotesque contention.

In a word, all the economic evidence tends to show that rationalisation carries with it a net diminution of employment, the substitution of a large proportion of low-skilled for high-skilled workers, and a distribution of the product which increases the proportionate share of Capital, reduces that of Labour.

CHAPTER VI

MARKETS AND DISTRIBUTION OF THE PRODUCT

§ The general progress of rationalisation consists in repressing competition and substituting unified control and management over production and finance in those industries that are most fundamental in relation to the needs of industry and life. Mining, transport, the textile, metal, oil, chemical and electrical industries, banking, insurance and finance, and an increasing number of agricultural operations, either in their productive or their marketing processes, furnish the chief examples of this movement.

But in order to secure the full economies of this process an expansion of markets equivalent to the increased productive capacity is admittedly required. This expansion of markets, however, is inhibited by the distribution of the product which rationalisation effects under uncontrolled Capitalism. For it enhances the proportion of the price which goes in profits, reduces that which goes in wages. So in accordance with our earlier analysis it prevents an adequate expansion of the market for the consumable goods which are the objective of rationalised production.

The progressive productivity of rationalisation cannot thus be achieved under a Capitalism which distributes the gains of its procedure so unfavourably for expansion of markets. This power of price-fixing, in order to make the maximum profits for the invested capital, must be controlled, if society is to obtain the fruits of this economy. For, as has been pointed out, there is no natural harmony between the price that yields the maximum profit and that which promotes the largest market. Once more we confront the problem of distribution of the 'surplus'. It may pay the private business to take in profit the whole of a smaller surplus by price-fixing, rather than to enlarge supply or lower prices so as to give to the consumer a lion's share of a larger surplus.

This is a problem of the public attitude towards monopoly. Here it is recognised that the State, as organ of the social interest, must take a hand. If we are dealing with a close monopoly in a vital industry, the alternative of private and public monopoly must normally be decided in favour of the latter. State and Municipal Socialism has in every civilised country been moving along this line. Railways, banks, mines, city lands, docks and harbours, local supplies, gas, water, electricity, etc., tend in most countries to become public services. There is, however, an element in 'rationalisation' which may be refractory to public management. Where the arts of scientific invention and of organisation are continually effecting new economies of cost, and are thus affording scope for individual initiative and adventure, it may well be held that public administration, even under such quasi-independent bodies as the Port of London Authority, is not the best way of securing for the people the fruits of the rationalising process. Two other methods are open: wage- and price-regulation and taxation, taken singly or in conjunction. Price-regulation, by itself, appears to involve great, if not insuperable, obstacles in some cases, as the War experience showed. For, unless full publicity and reliable cost-taking are available along the whole chain of processes from the extraction of raw materials through the transport, manufacturing and mercantile procedures, it is impossible to prescribe a 'reasonable' price which will be consistent with a full, reliable supply. This difficulty is illustrated in the complete failure of the attempts made in this country to tackle the growing margin in the final price of commodities taken in the distributive processes. Here, indeed, is one of the stiffest obstacles to a better distribution and an expansive market. Retail trades, by organised or separate refusal to hand on to consumers any adequate share of the fall in manufacturing and wholesale prices, are taking profits to which they have no reasonable claim, and are preventing that expansion of consumers' demand required to evoke full employment of capital and labour in the rationalised industries. This uncontrolled greed of the retailers is one of the major causes of our present economic discontents.

A surplus-profits tax so arranged as to stimulate supply and a low price-level would probably prove in many instances the best instrument, coupled with provisions for high wages, short hours, and other good conditions for employees in both the manufacturing and the distributive trades. In other words, it may be possible to leave to Capital a sufficient stimulus to push forward with its labour-saving economies, while securing to society the lion's share of the cost reduction. This policy has the double advantage of ensuring the largest volume of employment which rationalisation permits while so stimulating the expansion of markets as to encourage every new economy of rationalisation.

The lower price thus paid for the products of rationalised industries would raise the real income or purchasing power of consumers. It would enlarge the share of the workers in the social income, enabling them to consume a larger quantity of the rationalised products, or, alternatively, to apply a larger part of their wage-income to the purchase of other goods, thus stimulating employment and enlarging wage-income in the non-rationalised trades.[1]

---

[1] The new powers of compulsory enquiry and price-fixing attached to the appointment of the Consumers' Council form an important beginning to a procedure which may substitute an effective further control over industries deemed unsuitable for direct public operation.

CHAPTER VII

SOCIAL SERVICES AND WORKERS' INCOMES

§ In discussing the need for an adequate expansion of markets in order to preserve a true balance between productivity and consumption we have dwelt almost entirely upon the problem of distribution of the product, as between Capital and Labour, in profits and wages. Incidentally reference has been made to public expenditure upon services, such as pensions, insurance, unemployment doles, education, health, etc., which may be regarded as supplementary to wages, increasing the real income of the workers who are the main beneficiaries from these services. Indeed, many of these public aids come in a monetary form, directly adding to the spending power of the workers, while others relieve the workers' incomes from expenditure which otherwise would fall upon them. Many other publicly financed local services—cultural, recreational, hygienic, as well as transport—though available for all, are chiefly utilised by the worker and his family. So far as these services are supported, in whole or part, by rates or taxes, they must be reckoned as additions to the real incomes of the workers (due allowance being made for taxation borne by workers), an equalisation tendency in distribution of income.

This growth of social services mainly for the benefit of the workers was estimated by Professor Clay in 1925 as "equivalent to 12·5 per cent. on the total wages paid, or, including employers' contributions under Insurance Acts, 14.7 per cent". The total expenditure on social services rose from £22,600,000 in 1891 to £338,500,000 in 1925 (including war pensions).[1]

But even those public services not expressly designed for or utilised by the poorer classes, the expenditure on streets, lighting, public buildings, and other conveniences and amenities of civic life make for greater equality in distribution, inasmuch as their cost falls chiefly upon the well-to-do, while their benefits are equally

[1] The distribution of the totals is as follows:—

				£ millions 1891.	1925.
1.	Expenditure under	the Education Acts	..	11.5	89.4
2.	,,	,, Acts relating to the Relief of the Poor		9·1	40·4
3.	,,	,, the Housing Acts ..		0·2	18·4
4.	,,	,, the Public Health Acts..		0·5	9·1
5.	,,	,, the Lunacy and Mental Deficiency Acts ..		0·9	4·8
6.	,,	,, the National Health Insurance Acts		nil	32·5
7.	,,	,, the Unemployment Insurance Acts		nil	50·6
8.	,,	,, the War Pensions Acts ..		nil	66·5
9.	,,	,, the Old-Age Pensions Acts		nil	25·8
10.	Other Expenditure	.. ..		0·4	1·0
	Total £ millions	.. .. ..		22·6	338·5

divided. Or, putting the matter in another way, had those rates and taxes not been levied and applied to such public services, they would for the most part have swelled the incomes of the profit-making and other well-to-do classes, and a large part of them would have been applied, not to a demand for goods (consumable or capital goods), but to an attempt at saving more than the economic system is able to accommodate and utilise for production.

§ The extent of the redistribution of income thus achieved in favour of the workers depends, of course, upon the proportion of the contributions to the public revenue made by the workers and the well-to-do classes respectively. Of this no exact measurement is available, because there is no way of ascertaining what proportion of articles taxed under Customs and Excise are bought and consumed by the workers. But taking 1925 as a typical year, we find that the Imperial revenue from Customs and Excise amounted to £238 millions out of a total tax revenue of £690 millions and a total revenue of £779½ millions from all sources. Since motor-cars and other expensive luxuries figure more largely in Customs and Excise than formerly, it would be perhaps a fair guess to impute three-quarters of this indirect taxation to the working classes, or a sum of £169 millions as against the special benefits of £338 millions which they receive, as apart from the general benefits of Government in which they share. Here is a not inconsiderable shift in the distribution of the national income due to taxation. In this country, as in most others, there is a considerable tendency to raise a larger proportion of an increasing public revenue from progressive taxation of the incomes and property of the non-working classes, chiefly through income-tax, super-tax, and inheritance duties. And in most countries an increasing proportion of an enlarged public revenue is expended on social services in which the poorer classes are the main beneficiaries. This taxation, as also the high rating for local services, though it may sometimes be shown to increase costs of production in manufacturing and other businesses, tends to expand the total expenditure upon consumable goods and services, and so to stimulate production and employment.

The same reasoning is applicable, though in a less degree, to the public expenditure upon armed force, whether police or national defence. The taxation which sustains this expenditure is mainly drawn from income which, left in private hands, would either be expended upon luxuries or more largely would go to swell the already overfull saving and investment fund in periods of depressed trade. There is no sound reason in the lamentations over excessive taxation on the score that it adds to costs of production, raises prices, and restricts markets. Its real incidence is for the most part upon what we have termed surplus income and surplus property, in the sense that such income and property are not engaged in furnishing the costs of maintenance or of serviceable expansion of the productive factors. A large reduction of income-tax or inheritance duties, under existing circumstances, would for the most part go to enlarging the fund of saved or investable income which is already excessive, in that it cannot and does not quickly and easily pass into actual investment for the furtherance of production. There is no ground for holding that a reduction of such taxation would pass, to any considerable extent, in reduced costs of production and increased supplies of goods and lower prices to the consuming public, so as to raise the real income of the workers and increase the share of that income in the total income of the economic community.

Nor, *per contra*, is there reason to believe that a raising of such taxes would enable or oblige those who pay them to raise correspondingly the prices of the goods or services they sell, so passing on to the consumer the increased burden of taxation. There are, of course, limits to the 'capacity to pay', and where taxation so trenches upon interest and profits as to check the useful supply of capital and organising ability, that limit is passed. The general law of the incidence of taxation holds good that a tax imposed on rent of land, excess profits, or any monopoly or protected business, or upon inheritance, tends to lie where it is imposed and cannot be shifted, and that any tax not directly imposed upon such surpluses tends to shift from the 'cost' elements on which it is imposed, so as to settle upon the nearest surplus. This process of settlement by transfer is, however, sometimes slow and often expensive and disturbing, so that it is extremely important that taxation should, so far as possible, be directly imposed upon rents, quasi-rents, excess profits, and inheritances. A high progression in income-tax and death duties is justified as the most convenient method of estimating a true ability to pay, without disturbance to the productive services. Such taxation confers the double benefit of reducing the maldistribution of the real income of the economic community in favour of the workers, and thereby of procuring an expansion of markets which stimulates increased production by enlarging the employment of capital and labour.

§ The continuous increase in the proportion of the capital and income which in this and most advanced industrial communities is passing from private Capitalism into businesses owned, administrated, or regulated by the State or other public authority, testifies to an actual advance of 'Socialism'. Though this advance is due to a variety of causes, its chief effect is to promote a greater equality in distribution of incomes, offsetting the tendency of the new Capitalism to take an increasing share of the product in profits and managerial gains on account of the larger part played by capital as a productive factor.

In considering the total effect of taxation and public expenditure, it must not be forgotten that much of the money taken in taxes and rates is put to capital expenditure, thus ranking as national savings. The figure estimated by the Liberal Industrial Enquiry for 1926 amounts to £100 millions for Governmental expenditure (central and local), "including repayment of Government external debt, the Road Fund, telephones, and Local Loan Fund and capital expenditure by Local Authorities".

§ A more equal distribution of the product may thus come about, partly by higher wages for employees in public or private business undertakings; partly by lower prices for the goods produced which automatically raise the real wage, or purchasing power, of the whole body of workers as consumers; partly by taxation of profits or high incomes for pensions and other benefits to the workers. By such more equal distribution of purchasing power the tendency of rationalisation towards restricted output, price-fixing, high profits, and increasing unemployment (saved labour) can be counteracted. For the more unequal distribution of income as between capital and labour, which rationalisation with price-control brings about, would thus be remedied in two ways: first, by a better distribution of the product of the rationalised industries; secondly, by the restriction set upon rationalisation and its standardised mass-production by a raising of popular standards of living that will increase the demand for the finer and more individualised types of goods and services which in their production employ less capital and more skill than are needed in the rationalised industries.

By such methods it is conceivable that the new Capitalism, without any radical change in industrial government other than the possession or control of certain key industries by public authorities, might continue to operate. There is, however, one difficulty, the nature of which I have already indicated, which it may be impossible to overcome without a change of government within the several business organisations. This difficulty is the sole ownership of the business structure by those who own the capital part of that structure to the exclusion of any ownership vested in the active agents in the business, the workers with hand and brain. In other words, so long as the business is run primarily in the interests of the owners, and motived primarily or exclusively by the hope and expectation of profit, there is little security for the interests of the employees and the consumers, who, though vitally interested in the success of the business, have no voice in its control. There is in some quarters a growing disposition to acknowledge the 'rights' of the employees to a property in the business and a share in its direction. This is well expressed by the eminent economist, Mr. Owen D. Young, in a speech recently delivered at the opening of the new buildings of the Harvard School of Business Administration.

"I hope" (he said) "the day may come when these great business organisations will truly belong to the men who are giving their lives and their efforts to them. I care not in what capacity. They will then use capital truly as a tool, and they will be all interested in working it to the highest economic advantage. Then an idle machine will mean to every man in the plant who sees it an unproductive charge against himself. Then we shall have zest in labour, *provided the leadership be competent and the division fair.* Then we shall dispose once for all of the charge that in industry organisations are autocratic, not democratic. Then we shall have all the opportunities for a cultural wage which the business can provide. Then, in a word, men will be free in co-operative undertaking, and subject only to the same limitations and chances as men in individual businesses. Then we shall have no hired men."

§ But those who are watching carefully the development of great combines will not be satisfied with this harmony of interests and control, or with the substitution of a government by the workers for the autocracy of capital. In the success of such organisations there is a third factor: the market, the consuming public, whose interests and well-being might be jeopardised just as much by the business administration of the employees in a particular business as by that of the capitalist proprietors. The control of great combines by their employees might merely convert these employees into profiteers, whether they took their gains under the guise of high wages, or bonuses, or in some other way. It would be impossible for society to acquiesce in a price-fixing policy which either established groups of well-paid workers in strongly organised trades, battening through high prices on their weaker brother-workers, or which (as would probably follow) fomented incessant conflicts in the world of labour between combines and competitive trades, sheltered and unsheltered trades, key industries and industries producing non-essentials.

An equitable distribution of the product,

evoking full productivity through the best technique and the utmost economy of labour, and
providing for the absorption of all labour 'saved'
in standardised mass-production by a higher
general standard of consumption, which utilised
more labour in the finer arts of production,
would require a co-operation of all the economic
factors, including the consumer, in the regulation
of industry.

§ The consumer's interest must reconcile and
harmonise the otherwise conflicting pulls of the
several organised industries upon the product
of industry as a whole. It is only by devising
methods of diverting the surplus incomes from
the grip of strong groups of producers into the
service of the consumer that the general sense
of economic justice can be satisfied, and increasing productivity can be secured its necessary
expansion of markets. The identification of
business prosperity with high prices is a parti-
cularly perverse piece of obscurantism. The free
play of rising productivity can only distribute
its gains fairly through falling prices that represent reduced costs of production per item of the
increased goods. Any check to this process
signifies a conflict of 'pulls' or economic forces
in the processes of production or distribution.
Falling prices for goods, however, should not
entail falling wage-rates or salaries. Stabilised

money-incomes of producers would bring increases of real incomes through falling prices.
There is no reason why this fall of prices, due
to increased productivity, should be prevented
by an increase of money beyond what would be
needed to meet the larger wage and salary bills
which a full employment of labour and managerial
ability under full productivity would involve.
All attempts to distribute increased prosperity
between the Capital and Labour in the prospering trades without regard to consumers are inequitable and will remain constant causes of
economic friction and waste.

CHAPTER VIII

VITAL INCOME

§ As money-income finds its real significance in saleable goods and services, so this real income is finally expressed in terms of desirable life, in vital income. Ruskin was speaking not in terms of sentiment but of science when he said, "There is no wealth but life". Though economic wealth by no means covers the whole scope of human well-being, its final value or utility consists in the measure of its contribution to this well-being. Moreover, though there will be differences of opinion and of feeling as to the higher qualities of well-being, there will be a solid agreement as to the main contributions from economic resources. When Aristotle said that it was necessary first to have a livelihood and then to practise virtue, he talked plain sense. Now the goods and services, the product of our economic system, the real income, expand and shrink in terms of vital income according to the amount and character of the life which this 'real' income conveys in the processes of its production and consumption. In business book-keeping all productive activities rank as 'costs', all consumption as 'utility'. But in vital income no such sharp distinction is applicable. For productive activities are not all vital cost, or consumptive processes all vital utility. Some productive work is valued on its own account, some consumption is waste or 'illth'. Taking the mass of saleable goods and services in the 'real income', we must gather in the vital value from both sides of the economic process, setting the human gains against the human losses. We shall then find that the contribution made by our productive resources (our economic system) towards human welfare, the vital income, will vary, on the one hand, with the nature of the goods and services it produces, and, on the other with the distribution of the productive activities among the workers and the distribution of the product among the consumers. A given quantity of material wealth may thus vary almost infinitely in its vital cost of production, according as human skill and interest enter into the labour of its production, and the 'costly' tedium and toil are well- or ill-adjusted to the strength and character of different workers. Similarly, on the side of consumption, its vital utility will vary both with the nature of the consumables and with their distribution. The sound distribution of labour and of the product is broadly equalitarian, because most men have approximately the same needs, tastes, and enjoyments in respect of economic welfare. But this equalitarianism must rightly take due account of the difference in capacities for work and for enjoyment. It must conform, as far as is feasible, to the communist principle, "From each according to his powers, to each according to his needs".[1] The objection to attempts rigorously to impose this economic rule upon our economic system is that it assumes a human nature far more immediately responsive to the calls of justice and humanity than that which we actually find. It assumes that the best ethic of family life is available for the whole human family. But, because we cannot get this full measure of disinterested altruism and equity from men as we find them, that is no reason for not pressing forward along the road of equitable distribution as far as we can, making such allowances for egoistic greed and recalcitrance as we find necessary. To pretend that each man will do his best for equal pay with men whose 'best' is far less than his would be a foolishness that would injure the productivity of the economic system. But industrial society is moving visibly and not slowly along the road of distribution according to needs in the more urgent interpretation of that term. It has yet far to go, but it is important to realise that the farther it can go, the more valuable will be the reaction of this policy upon the productive processes. For though the lower needs of men, being identical or closely similar, are conformable to mass-production and the rationalising

[1] Or 'capacity to use'.

economy, the higher needs, expressing the individuality of the consumer, are to a less and less degree amenable to this economy, and call for labour of production which is more skilful, more interesting, and therefore less 'costly' in the vital sense.

§ This forecast of the possibilities of economic development for the furtherance of human values cannot, however, be accepted with complete assurance. It involves two conditions, neither of which may be sufficiently attainable. The first is the success of Labour and the consumer in taming the Leviathan of Capitalism to the social service by placing a bit upon its profiteering greed. The second, closely associated with the first, is the ability of a society, bred in the game of material accumulation and the prestige of material success, to extricate itself from this crude materialism.

The supreme test of our economic intelligence is our willingness and ability so to organise the use of our growing 'surplus' that, after the real needs of economic maintenance and progress have been met, the whole of the remainder may be directed to providing the economic support and the leisure needed for the general enlargement and enrichment of non-economic life. This problem is partly one of individual, partly one of public economy. Put succinctly, it is this.

Individuals must learn to check the inclination to take out in material luxury and other forms of malconsumption the increasing value of money-incomes which the new powers of production make possible, and to utilise a larger share of these powers in securing those higher goods and services which sustain the finer values and satisfactions. They must also purchase the 'opportunity of opportunities' called leisure by curbing the accumulation of material goods which, as J. S. Mill saw in his day, prevents all technical advances from adding to the ease and grace of human life. Mechanisation, standardisation, and rationalisation should fructify partly in larger masses of common goods for the common people, but partly also in larger leisure.

As a problem of public economy, the policy of utilising an increasing public revenue obtained by taxation or out of remunerative public undertakings for the provision of free services, protective, hygienic, educational, recreative to the community, assumes an ever-growing importance. Though it may be difficult to distinguish the economic from the non-economic yield of these services, more and more this public policy directs its expenditure to welfare, envisaged primarily in terms, not of economic, but of vital values. Thus more and more of the economic surplus comes, through individual and public policy, to nourish a personality and a community in which economic activities are involved, but in which they play a diminishing part. Schools and colleges, hospitals, public libraries, art galleries, parks, town-planning, and scores of other schemes for human betterment are destined to absorb an ever-increasing share of the economic income in what the older economists termed unproductive expenditure, but which, wisely directed, fulfil the wider human purpose subserved by the economic system.

This right proportion between economic maintenance, economic growth, and the economic support of extra-economic services is the widest aspect of the problem of distribution. In such degree as it is soluble, to that extent will economic waste and economic 'illth' disappear. A sound reorganisation of industry would secure full productivity and a maximum economic income, so distributed by its monetary instruments as to devote an ever-increasing share of the surplus over costs to the provision of leisure and the arts of life which need leisure for their cultivation. The possibility of such an achievement depends primarily upon getting more equality and equity into the operations of our economic system, especially into the marketing of goods and services by which individual incomes are determined, and into the province of public finance, by which the State, as representing the community, takes an increasing share of the income

which the political and economic activities of
the community have helped to make. Upon such
improvement in the use of surplus income depends
the full utilisation of those growing powers of
productivity which, though known to exist, are
not yet realisable because of maladjustments in
the distribution of income and of its expenditure.
What is needed is a fuller knowledge of the
workings of the system and a more conscious
guidance of economic forces in conformity with
attainable ideals of social welfare.

CHAPTER IX

ECONOMIC INTERNATIONALISM

§ As we have stated these principles of income and its uses, they are fully applicable only to a completely self-contained economic system, i.e. to the whole world of effective economic intercourse, or to some virtually self-contained nation. When we seek to apply them to nations whose members are in close marketing relations with the members of other nations, or where considerable freedom of migration exists, modifications and retardations in the application of these principles are inevitable. An illustration is furnished by the contrast between the present condition of employment in France and in Britain. France, still a semi-industrialised country, with less inequality of incomes than Britain, a rigorously controlled growth of population, and an obstructive tariff system which makes her less dependent than most other advanced countries upon economic intercourse with outside areas, has virtually no unemployed capital and labour. Britain, more fully industrialised, dependent upon outside markets for essential foods and many raw materials, and for the disposal of her growing output of manufactures, and with a still growing population, is confronted with an apparently insoluble problem of unemployment.

If there were free trade, free mobility of capital and labour, throughout the economic world, with more effective international banking and finance, it seems to some economists that full employment, maximum productivity, and such a distribution of the 'surplus' as would satisfy all reasonable claims of equity and humanity would ensue. But to the attainment of any such ideals there are two related obstacles. The first is an uncontrolled industrialism under new conditions of technique and organisation spreading rapidly through hitherto backward and undeveloped countries. The second is a continuing rapid increase of world population, of which a growing proportion consists of coloured peoples adaptable to labour under white control and at low rates of real wages.

Now, here enters a new possibility of danger, which elsewhere I have designated Inter-imperialism, an economic international co-operation of advanced industrial peoples for the exploitation of the labour and the undeveloped natural resources of backward countries, chiefly in Africa and Asia. It would be feasible for the Capitalist groups in the advanced countries to suspend their costly struggles for areas of exploitation, conducted with the forced aid of their respective Governments, and accompanied, as a costly by-product, by great and little wars, and to work in friendly co-operation for the common exploitation of these backward countries and their peoples. Such an international economic policy easily emerges from a growth of international Cartels in many fields. Oil, copper, rubber, cotton, and a growing number of raw materials point to the progress of such international operations, conducted with the connivance or active support of the several Governments whose group-interests are involved.

There is a growing disposition to move in this direction on the part of Big Business threatened by the growing Trade Unionism and political power of white workers. Why should not labour troubles caused by white workers and their socialistic legislation be bought off by high wages and other good conditions at the expense of the backward peoples? Thus the economic division of interests might take a new shape. For the cleavage between Capital and Labour, or strong and weak industries, in the Western World might be substituted a less dangerous division. But, regarding the economic system as a whole, this policy could only hope to ease the immediate situation in the West. It could offer no final remedy to the disease of an inadequate expansion of markets due to maldistribution of purchasing power. It could only alter the shape of the problem. A world-commerce system conducted under such conditions would retain and very probably enhance the inequality of income which, as we have seen, disables effective demand for commodities from keeping pace with the increase of the industrial producing power. Nothing short of a continuous advance in the consuming power of the great, new backward peoples with their increasing numbers could find adequate employment for the constant advances of productive power in the countries equipped with modern methods of manufacture.

§ But since neither in a competitive industrial system nor in the new cartelised system which presses to take its place is there any reasonable hope of developing a price and wage system which shall stimulate adequately this advance of effective demand in backward countries, we appear to be faced with a continual recurrence of cycles of grave depression in the manufacturing industries of the advanced countries, and their familiar reactions upon finance, commerce, and agriculture. It is these experiences, and fears of their repetition, that drive most industrial nations into protection in a vain effort to retain a home market adequate to the demands of the new productive technique. The effort must be vain, for even if this protective system brought a rising standard of wages for a controlled population, that rising standard could not keep pace with the growing productivity of manufactures. An industrial country cannot in the long run live on its home market. It must continually seek more foreign areas in which to buy and sell and invest and develop.

Some alleviation of this situation is, however, possible. So far as a greater equalisation of income in an industrialised country is attainable, either by Trade Union organisation (with restriction on the growth of workers' families), or by political action in the shape of minimum wages and maximum hours regulations, or by public subsidies levied upon surplus income, the otherwise wasteful elements of surplus can be converted into human welfare. So far as this equalisation of income stimulates consumption, and reduces the proportion of attempted material 'saving', it will furnish larger employment for industrial resources, employing more of the new saving at home and exporting less of it. This more equal distribution of income would thus reduce the proportion of income saved, though not necessarily the amount of saving. For the total product and income would be larger. It would tend to restrict the pace of growth of industrial capital by diverting much of the potential new industrial capital to direct human consumption, either as personal income or as social welfare. This policy would bring a fuller use of productive resources, greater total productivity, and greater human benefit from the larger aggregate income, or from its substitute, the larger leisure.

But though a single nation, like Britain, might put into operation this improved economy with some benefit, it could not get or retain the full human or economic gain, unless some corresponding movement towards equalisation of incomes and enlargement of consuming powers was taking place in all or most other countries forming integral parts of the world-economic system. For if in a single country, e.g. Britain, this policy were in operation, new capital would tend to flow into other countries where a sweating economy was still feasible. Penalties or prohibitions upon such enlarged export of capital, if effective, would make for an isolated economic state which, in the case of Britain, might bring such impoverishment that a better distribution of the reduced product would not yield a net gain of welfare.

So far as free mobility of flow of capital and goods exists, it is impossible to guarantee full employment in a single country. If labour were as mobile as capital, actual unemployment might not occur. What would happen would be that less productive work was done in some national areas, more in others, for the benefit of the world-economic system. But labour continues to be far less mobile than capital. This is partly because labour consists of labourers, human beings with attachments and interests outside the economic sphere, who are not willing to place themselves indifferently in any part of the world where higher wages call them. Still more potent are the obstacles put upon free immigration in countries where organised labour can conserve its superior economic status by legal restrictions upon entrance into its sphere.

§ These considerations make it evident that full productivity and employment can only be attainable in such a country as Britain by a combination of two lines of economic policy. An internal policy of higher wages and of taxation directed to secure for public expenditure a larger share of rents and other surplus incomes would, by increasing the current consumption or demand for commodities, at once permit fuller employment of all existing productive resources, and stimulate employers and their brain-workers to discover and apply the best methods of technique and organisation. It is possible that this policy, boldly pursued, might so reduce costs of production per unit of the product in industry and agriculture as might not only hold the home market against foreign competition in manufactured goods, but also secure so large an export market as to pay for all the larger importations of food and raw materials which the enlarged consumption of our population would require. On this hypothesis we could, out of the better use of our own hands and brains, by a policy of better internal distribution, so raise our productivity as to secure economic health and progress without external assistance. But this assumes that other industrial nations are not cutting their costs of production by operating the new technique without any corresponding measures for the better and more equal distribution of consuming power. A policy of low wages, long hours, and low taxation in other industrial countries competing with us in the world-market might still enable them to secure so large a share of the limited[1] world-market as to continue to restrict the output of our export trades.

§ It is essential that Labour in this country should recognise the limitations of a High-Wage Short-Hours policy for our workers. In every industry there are obvious limits to 'the economy of high wages' in the promotion of efficiency. Though it is true that in America high wages, established during times when there was a relative shortage of hired labour, have been both cause and effect of efficient machine production, in Germany and other Continental countries high technical equipment is operated on a definitely lower wage and hours standard. Our recent losses of important foreign markets are

[1] i.e. limited by the failure of world-markets to keep pace with the rising powers of world-production.

undoubtedly attributable in part to the lower costs of labour in nations competing for a limited world-market. Under such conditions it will not be possible for us to maintain a standard of living much higher than that of our trade competitors. This would be realised more clearly if the final irrelevance of political barriers to trade were not obscured by tariffs and other false pretences that nations are trading with one another. It is only individual businesses or individual men who conduct trade. Everybody is aware that, if some English firms in a competitive business can get cheaper labour than other English firms, it is an advantage to them in getting contracts within this country. It is just as certain that, if these English firms are competing with foreign firms for contracts, the lower labour-costs of the foreigners will help them to outbid our firms. When low wages are accompanied by inferior capital equipment, the lower wage-bill may be offset by the inferior plant. But where technique and organisation are combined with lower wage-rates, as in Germany, it is foolish to suppose that legal or Trade Union action can maintain wages in this country at a definitely higher level. They can do so in the sheltered trades but at the expense of the unsheltered, and with ever-growing difficulty in exporting goods enough to pay for the foreign goods and materials we require, and in taking our part in the development of backward countries. That this last function is far less important than before has already been admitted. Other nations, America in particular, can afford to export capital in larger quantities for world-development. Moreover, the approaching stabilisation of our population reduces the importance of providing increased funds of foreign food and materials.

Nevertheless, we cannot afford to shut our eyes to the fact that our world-trade supremacy has gone and is irrecoverable. Rationalisation may help us to recover some foreign markets, but not if it is accompanied by wage-standards that disregard those of well-equipped foreign competitors. If, as there is no doubt, large bodies of surplus profits, rents, and other un-earned incomes exist in this country, taxation is a better instrument for a social policy of utilising them than wage-raising. For wage-raising in a competitive trade destroys the weaker businesses, and enables the surviving stronger ones to raise the price of the product, either by combination or by the reduction of supply due to the elimination of the weaker businesses. A progressive profit-tax has no such effect, and simply diverts to public revenue and social services what the trade can afford to pay. The pressure for expansion in our foreign market more and more takes the shape of seeking trade in backward countries, and is a struggle for this trade with exporters from countries that were once our customers. That enormous potential markets exist in Africa, China, and elsewhere there can be no doubt, but the expansion of these markets requires a complete reversal of the economic exploitation that has hitherto prevailed in the relations between advanced and backward countries. So long as a large part of the food and raw materials raised in tropical and other backward, non-industrial countries is the product of ill-paid or servile labour, the low consumption of imported manufactures in these countries will serve as a real restraint upon the productivity and full employment of the manufacturing trades in the exporting nations. A policy of better distribution of income in this country requires, therefore, to be supported by a corresponding movement in other countries, both those in direct competition with us as exporters of manufactured goods and those which produce the foods and raw materials we require, and receive in payment our manufactures.

§ Thus we reach the conclusion of our argument. The world is in effect a single economic system, and the improved or impaired productivity and consumption of every part affects every other part. Closer and more effective international movements for such improvements in the distri-

ECONOMIC INTERNATIONALISM 125

bution of income as will enable world consumption to keep pace with and stimulate improvements in production, form the foundation of the progressive economy and the humaner civilisation of the future. This can only be achieved by carrying the principle of rationalisation a step farther. So far it has striven to organise as productive and selling instruments single industries or groups of industries (by lateral or horizontal extension) in single countries or in the industrial world. But these rationalised groups are sovereign independent economic states, liable to prey upon one another and upon the less-organised industries in the different countries. Moreover, this rationalisation, conducted primarily for profit, is found to promote a distribution of purchasing power unequal to that required in the joint interests of the rationalised industries. Therefore, this procedure, operated by private Capitalism in the interest of profits, requires to be brought under a social control which must in the long run be international, so as to correspond with the area of the economic system itself. This economic internationalism, the forms of which it is perhaps premature to discuss, derives from the growing recognition of the fact that the modern powers of production can only be utilised by a government of industry consciously directed to secure for all a rising standard of life in which increasing leisure and non-economic values shall be the fruits of rationalisation. How far and how fast this conception of the part to be played by the economic system in a world-civilisation is realisable constitutes the most challenging problem of our age.

T - #0032 - 230425 - C0 - 216/138/7 [9] - CB - 9780415687867 - Gloss Lamination